MW00886955

Liability Disclaimer for Use of the Sigma Trust

The information, advice, and materials provided in this book, including the **Sigma Trust** structure and its components, are for informational purposes only and are not intended as legal, financial, or professional advice. While the author and publisher have made every effort to ensure the accuracy and completeness of the information, they do not warrant or guarantee the results from using the **Sigma Trust** or any other strategy described herein.

No Legal, Financial, or Tax Advice:

The **Sigma Trust** structure and its applications are complex legal entities that may have significant legal, tax, and financial implications. Readers are strongly advised to consult with a qualified legal, tax, or financial professional before taking any actions based on the information provided in this book. The use of the **Sigma Trust** structure may vary depending on jurisdiction, personal circumstances, and applicable laws.

No Guarantee of Results:

There is no guarantee that following the strategies outlined in this book will result in the protection of assets, tax exemptions, or other desired outcomes. Each individual's situation is unique, and the success of implementing the **Sigma Trust** or any related trust structure will depend on numerous factors, including but not limited to local laws, court decisions, and actions taken by administrative agencies.

Indemnification:

By using the **Sigma Trust** or any related strategy, the user agrees to indemnify and hold harmless the author, publisher, and associated entities from any claims, losses, damages, liabilities, or costs (including legal fees) arising out of or in connection with the use of the information provided in this book.

Administrative Agency Risks:

The **Sigma Trust** is designed to offer asset protection and safeguard against various legal risks, but there is no certainty that administrative agencies or other entities will not challenge, intervene in, or otherwise interfere with the operation of the trust. Users of the **Sigma Trust** should be aware that the legal and regulatory environment is subject to change, and no structure can offer complete immunity from legal or administrative actions.

No Liability for Fraud, Abuse, or Legal Action:

The author and publisher are not responsible for any fraudulent, illegal, or improper use of the **Sigma Trust**. It is the responsibility of the user to ensure that the trust and its assets are managed in accordance with all applicable laws, regulations, and ethical standards. The author and publisher disclaim any liability for legal disputes, fraud, abuse, or challenges that arise as a result of using the information in this book.

Conclusion:

By using the **Sigma Trust** or any of the strategies discussed in this book, the user acknowledges and agrees to the terms of this liability disclaimer. It is the responsibility of the user to seek appropriate legal, tax, and financial guidance tailored to their individual circumstances. The author and publisher make no representations or warranties as to the effectiveness, legality, or outcomes of using the **Sigma Trust** structure or any associated strategies.

Book Title

"The Sigma Trust Blueprint: Asset Protection, Sovereignty, and Legacy"

Chapter 1: The Foundation of the Sigma Trust

Section 1: Understanding Trusts: Revocable vs. Irrevocable
Section 2: The Genesis of the Sigma Trust: A New Paradigm
Section 3: Core Principles: Asset Protection, Tax Efficiency, and Sovereignty
Section 4: Legal Framework and the Role of Irrevocability

Chapter 2: The Threefold Capacity Framework

Section 1: Principal, Agent, and Trustee: The Trinity of Roles
Section 2: Understanding Multi-Capacity Functions
Section 3: How Each Role Protects the Trust and Assets
Section 4: Case Studies of Multi-Capacity Implementation

Chapter 3: Funding the Sigma Trust

Section 1: Initial Funding: Transferring Assets into the Trust
Section 2: Continuous Contributions: Donations, Royalties, and Income Streams
Section 3: Strategic Asset Placement: Intellectual Property, Investments, and More
Section 4: Transferring Social Security Benefits Without Waiting

Chapter 4: Asset Protection Strategies

Section 1: Shielding the Trust from Administrative Agencies
Section 2: Protecting Intellectual Property: Trademarks and Copyrights
Section 3: Legal Safeguards Against Fraudulent Claims
Section 4: Building a Firewall Against Creditors and Third-Party Claims

Chapter 5: Tax Strategies and Legal Compliance

Section 1: The Sigma Trust and Tax Exemption
Section 2: Navigating Tax Laws and Reporting Requirements
Section 3: Tax Efficiency Through Trust Management
Section 4: Avoiding Legal Pitfalls and Ensuring Compliance

Chapter 6: Intellectual Property Management

Section 1: Assigning Copyrights, Trademarks, and Royalties to the Trust
Section 2: Monetizing Intellectual Property Through the Trust
Section 3: Legal Protections Against Copyright Infringement
Section 4: Growing Intellectual Property Assets

Chapter 7: Managing Income and Distributions

Section 1: The Trustee's Role in Managing Income Streams
Section 2: Balancing Distributions: Beneficiaries vs. Principal's Needs
Section 3: Protecting the Principal's Lifestyle Through the Trust
Section 4: Ethical Considerations in Managing Trust Income

Chapter 8: Safeguarding Against Administrative Fraud

Section 1: Legal Protections Embedded in the Sigma Trust
Section 2: Administrative Fraud Tactics and How to Counteract Them
Section 3: Using the Trust Protector for Oversight and Defense
Section 4: Building an Anti-Fraud Infrastructure

Chapter 9: Clauses, Protections, and Authenticity

Section 1: Key Clauses to Strengthen the Sigma Trust
Section 2: Authenticity Mechanisms: Preventing Fraudulent Misuse of the Trust
Section 3: Advanced Protection Strategies for Assets and Intellectual Property
Section 4: Customizing the Sigma Trust for Maximum Flexibility

Chapter 10: Legacy Planning and Long-Term Goals

Section 1: Ensuring the Trust's Continuity Beyond Your Lifetime
Section 2: Designating Successor Trustees and Beneficiaries
Section 3: Passing Down Intellectual Property Rights and Assets
Section 4: How the Sigma Trust Creates Generational Wealth

Chapter 11: Building a Movement with the Sigma Trust

Section 1: Using the Sigma Trust as a Tool for Sovereignty
Section 2: Inspiring Others to Build Their Own Trusts
Section 3: The Sigma Trust as a Model for Social and Economic Reform
Section 4: Final Thoughts: Securing Your Legacy with Confidence

Appendices

- **Appendix A:** Sample Trust Agreement Template
- **Appendix B:** Glossary of Key Terms
- **Appendix C:** Recommended Resources and Tools
- **Appendix D:** Case Studies and Success Stories

Chapter 1: The Foundation of the Sigma Trust

Section 1: Understanding Trusts: Revocable vs. Irrevocable

Trusts are among the most versatile and secure tools for estate planning, asset management, and legal protection. However, choosing the appropriate type of trust is essential to meet specific goals such as asset protection, tax efficiency, or legacy planning. The two primary types of trusts—**revocable** and **irrevocable**—differ significantly in terms of control, flexibility, and protection. Understanding these differences is critical for establishing a robust legal framework like the Sigma Trust.

Revocable Trusts: Flexible Estate Planning

A **revocable trust**, often referred to as a "living trust," is designed to offer flexibility and control. The grantor (the person creating the trust) retains full control over the trust's terms and assets, allowing them to:

1. **Amend or revoke the trust**: Modify the terms or dissolve the trust entirely at any time.
2. **Manage assets**: The grantor can act as the trustee, overseeing the trust property directly.
3. **Avoid probate**: Upon the grantor's death, assets in the trust transfer directly to beneficiaries without court involvement.

While revocable trusts provide ease of management and probate avoidance, they do not offer protection from creditors or legal claims. Assets in a revocable trust remain part of the grantor's taxable estate, meaning they are exposed to estate taxes and legal liability.

Irrevocable Trusts: Asset Protection and Sovereignty

An **irrevocable trust** operates on a stricter framework. Once created, the grantor generally cannot modify or revoke the trust without the consent of beneficiaries or legal authorization. This relinquishment of control is precisely what makes irrevocable trusts a powerful legal tool:

1. **Asset protection**: Assets transferred to the trust are no longer owned by the grantor, shielding them from creditors, lawsuits, or administrative actions.

2. **Tax benefits**: Because the grantor relinquishes ownership, assets in an irrevocable trust are excluded from their taxable estate, reducing potential estate and income tax liabilities.

3. **Legal independence**: The trust's assets and operations are protected from interference by external entities, provided the trust is properly structured and legally compliant.

It is essential to carefully plan the establishment and funding of an irrevocable trust to ensure compliance with federal, state, and local laws. Mismanagement or improper use can expose the trust to legal challenges.

The Sigma Trust: Advanced Irrevocability

The **Sigma Trust** adopts the principles of irrevocability while integrating modern safeguards and innovative management structures. It redefines traditional irrevocable trusts by embedding flexibility through legally accepted mechanisms, ensuring compliance and adaptability. Key features include:

- **Multi-role capacities**: Allowing the grantor to act in legally distinct roles such as principal, trustee, or agent within clear boundaries.
- **Funding mechanisms**: Donations, royalties, and income streams can be transferred into the trust through lawful and documented means.
- **Comprehensive asset protection**: Safeguards that adhere to existing laws, shielding the trust from creditors and administrative interference.

The Sigma Trust is designed to operate within the framework of legal protections while maximizing the benefits of irrevocability.

Why Choose an Irrevocable Trust for Asset Protection?

For individuals seeking to protect assets from external risks, irrevocable trusts are the preferred legal solution. By transferring ownership to the trust, the grantor creates a secure environment for wealth and intellectual property, ensuring long-term stability and protection.

However, establishing an irrevocable trust must be executed carefully to comply with applicable laws. Transparency, proper documentation, and adherence to fiduciary duties are essential to avoiding accusations of fraud, tax evasion, or improper asset transfers.

The **Sigma Trust** is designed as a lawful and ethical tool to provide robust protection, operational clarity, and legacy-building potential. By prioritizing legality and accountability, it ensures that the trust remains impervious to legal challenges while serving its purpose.

Chapter 1: The Foundation of the Sigma Trust

Section 2: The Genesis of the Sigma Trust: A New Paradigm

The Sigma Trust represents a transformative approach to asset protection, estate planning, and personal sovereignty. It is not merely a legal entity; it is a paradigm shift in how individuals safeguard their legacy, intellectual property, and wealth against external threats. The Sigma Trust transcends traditional trust structures by integrating innovative frameworks that prioritize legal compliance, ethical governance, and strategic adaptability.

The Conceptual Birth of the Sigma Trust

The Sigma Trust was conceived out of the need for a more dynamic and protective trust structure. Traditional irrevocable trusts, while robust, often lack flexibility and adaptability. On the other hand, revocable trusts are too vulnerable to external claims. The Sigma Trust bridges this gap by creating a legally compliant and ethically sound structure that offers the following:

1. **Total asset shielding**: Protection against creditors, administrative agencies, and legal liabilities.
2. **Sovereign identity management**: Legal ownership and protection of intellectual property, including names, trademarks, copyrights, and royalties.
3. **Strategic funding mechanisms**: Seamlessly integrating donations, royalties, and other revenue streams as part of a cohesive framework.

The Sigma Trust introduces a multi-capacity governance model, leveraging the roles of principal, trustee, and agent to create a resilient system for managing assets and responsibilities.

The Multi-Capacity Framework

At the heart of the Sigma Trust lies its multi-capacity framework, which redefines the roles traditionally associated with trust management:

1. **Principal**: Represents the originator of the trust, who transfers ownership of assets to the trust. The principal establishes the intent and purpose of the trust and may contribute intellectual property, royalties, or other assets.
2. **Trustee**: Acts as the legal steward of the trust's assets, ensuring they are managed according to the terms of the trust. The trustee may be an individual, a corporate entity, or a structured fiduciary body.
3. **Agent**: Serves as the operational executor, carrying out specific functions such as asset acquisition, revenue generation, and external negotiations.

This layered structure ensures that the Sigma Trust remains legally insulated while maintaining operational efficiency and strategic flexibility.

The Sigma Trust is not merely an adaptation of existing models; it introduces several groundbreaking innovations:

1. **Sovereign intellectual property**: The trust owns and manages the intellectual property of the grantor, including their name, likeness, and creative works. This safeguards against misuse and ensures royalties flow directly into the trust.

2. **Religious framework integration**: By aligning its governance structure with a religious or spiritual paradigm (e.g., principal as God, trustee as Spirit, and agent as Body), the Sigma Trust creates additional ethical and legal layers of protection.

3. **Cestui Que Vie principles**: Utilizing historical legal doctrines, the Sigma Trust incorporates protections typically reserved for sovereign entities, ensuring assets are managed and shielded from administrative overreach.

The Sigma Trust as a New Paradigm

The Sigma Trust represents a shift from reactive asset protection to proactive sovereignty. By emphasizing long-term security, ethical governance, and legal resilience, it empowers individuals to operate beyond the limitations of traditional financial and legal systems.

This new paradigm is designed to:

- Provide **immunity** from unnecessary administrative interference.
- Establish a **legacy structure** that protects assets for future generations.
- Uphold **ethical and legal integrity**, ensuring compliance with all applicable laws while maximizing autonomy.

The Sigma Trust is not just a financial tool; it is a statement of independence and responsibility, embodying the principles of self-determination and justice.

A Vision for the Future

The Sigma Trust sets a new standard in trust creation and management. By integrating traditional principles with modern innovations, it offers a robust and legally secure path forward for those seeking to protect their legacy and ensure their sovereignty.

Chapter 1: The Foundation of the Sigma Trust

Section 3: Core Principles: Asset Protection, Tax Efficiency, and Sovereignty

The Sigma Trust is built upon three core principles: **asset protection**, **tax efficiency**, and **sovereignty**. Each principle serves as a pillar that supports the trust's primary purpose: to create a legally secure and ethically sound structure for managing wealth, intellectual property, and personal autonomy. These principles are intricately woven into the trust's design, ensuring it functions as a robust tool for long-term stability and resilience.

1. Asset Protection

Asset protection is the cornerstone of the Sigma Trust. In an era where individuals face increasing threats from creditors, lawsuits, and administrative overreach, the Sigma Trust provides a secure legal framework to shield assets from external claims.

Key Features of Asset Protection

- **Ownership Transfer**: Assets are legally transferred to the trust, removing them from the personal estate of the grantor. This separation creates a barrier that protects the assets from being targeted in legal disputes or debt collection.
- **Creditor Shielding**: Once assets are within the Sigma Trust, they are generally inaccessible to creditors, provided the transfer was done in compliance with fraudulent transfer laws.
- **Administrative Immunity**: The Sigma Trust is structured to minimize interference from

administrative agencies, safeguarding
against unjust taxation or confiscation.

Applications

1. Intellectual Property: The trust owns
   copyrights, trademarks, and patents,
   ensuring their protection against
   unauthorized use.
2. Physical Assets: Real estate, vehicles, and
   other tangible property are secured within
   the trust to protect against lawsuits or liens.
3. Financial Assets: Bank accounts, investment
   portfolios, and other financial instruments are
   shielded from personal liabilities.

2. Tax Efficiency

The Sigma Trust is designed to optimize tax efficiency
while maintaining strict compliance with tax laws. By
leveraging the unique advantages of irrevocable trusts, it

ensures that assets and income are managed in a way that minimizes tax liabilities.

Key Tax Benefits

- **Exclusion from Taxable Estate**: Assets within the trust are no longer considered part of the grantor's taxable estate, potentially reducing estate taxes.
- **Income Tax Optimization**: Depending on the trust's structure, income generated by trust assets can be distributed to beneficiaries in lower tax brackets or retained within the trust to take advantage of favorable tax treatment.
- **Charitable Deductions**: Donations to the trust may qualify as tax-deductible contributions, further enhancing tax efficiency.

Ethical Compliance

While the Sigma Trust provides significant tax benefits, it prioritizes transparency and adherence to all applicable tax regulations. Ethical compliance ensures the trust remains secure from legal challenges and audits.

3. Sovereignty

Sovereignty is the defining principle that sets the Sigma Trust apart from conventional trust structures. It empowers individuals to regain control over their wealth and legacy, free from unnecessary interference by external entities.

Personal Sovereignty

The Sigma Trust aligns with the principle of individual sovereignty by:

- Providing complete control over the terms and governance of the trust.
- Enabling the grantor to establish a legacy that reflects their values and vision.
- Protecting the grantor's intellectual and personal property, including their name and likeness.

Legal Sovereignty

The trust operates within the boundaries of the law while maintaining a structure that minimizes vulnerabilities:

- **Multi-Capacity Governance**: By assigning distinct roles (principal, trustee, agent), the Sigma Trust creates a system of checks and balances that enhances its resilience.
- **Cestui Que Vie Principles**: Leveraging historical doctrines, the trust reinforces its sovereignty by ensuring its assets are treated as distinct and independent from the grantor's personal estate.

Community Sovereignty

When combined with religious or ethical principles (e.g., God as the principal, Spirit as the trustee, and Body as the agent), the trust integrates a deeper sense of purpose and accountability, aligning its operations with higher values.

The Intersection of the Core Principles

The Sigma Trust's design ensures that asset protection, tax efficiency, and sovereignty are not isolated objectives but interconnected elements that reinforce one another. This synergy creates a trust that is:

- **Legally Robust**: Operating within the framework of established laws to ensure long-term stability.
- **Ethically Sound**: Upholding principles of justice and transparency in all its functions.
- **Practically Resilient**: Adaptable to changing legal and financial landscapes without compromising its foundational goals.

Conclusion

The core principles of asset protection, tax efficiency, and sovereignty form the bedrock of the Sigma Trust. By prioritizing these principles, the trust establishes itself as a revolutionary tool for securing wealth, protecting intellectual property, and empowering individuals to reclaim their autonomy.

In the next section, we will delve deeper into the mechanics of funding the trust, exploring how donations, royalties, and other revenue streams can be integrated into its structure to ensure sustainability and growth.

Chapter 1: The Foundation of the Sigma Trust

Section 4: Legal Framework and the Role of Irrevocability

The Sigma Trust's strength lies in its irrevocable nature and carefully constructed legal framework. These elements provide the trust with the stability, security, and protection necessary to fulfill its purpose. This section outlines the legal principles underpinning the trust and explains how irrevocability safeguards assets, ensures compliance, and fortifies its sovereignty.

Understanding the Legal Framework

A trust is a legal relationship in which the grantor transfers assets to a trustee to be managed for the benefit of designated beneficiaries. The Sigma Trust expands this concept by integrating advanced legal doctrines and protections.

Key Elements of the Legal Framework

1. **Irrevocability**: Once the trust is established, the grantor cannot unilaterally revoke or amend its terms. This ensures the trust remains legally independent and protects its assets.
2. **Separation of Roles**: By clearly defining the roles of the principal, trustee, and agent, the Sigma Trust ensures transparency and mitigates conflicts of interest.

3. **Compliance with Statutory Laws**: The trust is constructed to operate within existing legal and regulatory frameworks, ensuring it is both enforceable and resilient against challenges.
4. **Asset Segregation**: Assets transferred to the trust are no longer considered the personal property of the grantor, insulating them from creditors and legal claims.

The Role of Irrevocability

The irrevocability of the Sigma Trust is one of its defining features, offering both legal and practical benefits.

Key Advantages of Irrevocability

1. **Legal Protection**:
   - **Asset Shielding**: Irrevocability prevents assets from being claimed

by creditors or administrative
agencies.

- o **Litigation Immunity**: Since the grantor relinquishes control over the assets, they are less likely to be targeted in lawsuits.
- o **Preservation of Intent**: The terms and conditions of the trust cannot be easily altered, ensuring that the grantor's original purpose is honored.

2. **Tax Efficiency**:

- o **Estate Tax Exemption**: Assets in an irrevocable trust are not included in the grantor's taxable estate.
- o **Income Tax Optimization**: Depending on the structure, the trust may have favorable tax treatment for income and capital gains.

3. **Sovereignty and Independence**:

- o **Autonomy**: Irrevocability ensures the trust operates independently of the grantor's personal circumstances.

- Administrative Protection: The trust's irrevocable nature limits administrative agencies' ability to interfere or make claims.

Balancing Irrevocability with Flexibility

While irrevocability provides significant protections, it is often viewed as rigid. The Sigma Trust addresses this by incorporating flexible mechanisms within the bounds of the law.

Key Features for Flexibility

1. Defined Powers for the Trustee: The trustee is granted discretionary powers to adapt the management of assets in response to changing circumstances.
2. Appointment of Successor Trustees: The trust allows for the replacement of trustees to ensure proper administration.

3. **Beneficiary Amendments**: While the trust terms are irrevocable, provisions may allow adjustments to the distribution of assets to beneficiaries under specific conditions.
4. **Special Purpose Clauses**: These clauses allow the trust to respond to external changes, such as tax law amendments or new regulatory requirements.

Irrevocability and Ethical Considerations

The irrevocable nature of the Sigma Trust must align with ethical practices. It is designed to:

- Ensure transparency in its formation and operation.
- Avoid fraudulent transfers by adhering to laws governing asset transfers.
- Honor the intent of the grantor while protecting the rights of beneficiaries.

By maintaining ethical integrity, the trust minimizes legal risks and strengthens its standing in court if ever challenged.

Historical and Legal Foundations of Irrevocability

Irrevocable trusts are rooted in centuries of legal tradition, from English common law to modern statutory frameworks. These principles emphasize the sanctity of the trust's terms and the importance of fiduciary responsibility.

Key Doctrines Supporting Irrevocability

1. **Cestui Que Vie Principles**: These principles recognize the trust as a distinct legal entity, separate from the grantor.
2. **Fiduciary Duty**: Trustees are legally bound to act in the best interests of the beneficiaries, ensuring the trust is managed responsibly.
3. **Contract Law**: The trust's irrevocability is enforced as a binding contract between the

grantor and the trustee, with clear terms and conditions.

Conclusion

The Sigma Trust's legal framework and irrevocable nature are fundamental to its effectiveness. By ensuring that assets are legally protected, tax-efficient, and sovereign, the trust creates a robust structure that upholds the grantor's intent while providing flexibility within defined parameters.

In the next chapter, we will explore the funding mechanisms of the Sigma Trust, detailing how donations, royalties, and other income streams are integrated into the trust to ensure its sustainability and growth.

Chapter 2: The Threefold Capacity
Framework

Section 1: Executor, Trustee, and Beneficiary: The Trinity of Roles in the Sigma Trust

The Sigma Trust operates on a groundbreaking threefold capacity framework, where the roles of Executor, Trustee, and Beneficiary are infused with unique spiritual and practical significance. These roles reflect the integration of divine principles, legal mechanics, and human agency to create a trust structure that is both sovereign and resilient.

The Threefold Framework

1. **Executor**: Representing ultimate authority, the Executor embodies the divine (God) and establishes the trust's purpose and direction.
2. **Trustee**: The Trustee, guided by the spirit, serves as the operational manager and steward of the trust.
3. **Beneficiary**: The Beneficiary, symbolized by the body, reaps the benefits of the trust's assets and services.

This framework intertwines spiritual and legal capacities, creating a trust that functions holistically across different planes of existence.

Role 1: The Executor (God)

The Executor is the creator and sovereign authority of the Sigma Trust. This role represents the divine principle that underpins the trust, establishing it as an instrument of higher purpose and sovereignty.

Responsibilities of the Executor:

- Declaring the trust's intent, mission, and principles.
- Naming the Trustee and defining their powers.
- Ensuring the trust adheres to its divine and ethical foundations.
- Overseeing the trust's ultimate purpose, which transcends material goals.

Advantages of the Executor Role:

- Provides the trust with sovereign authority, protecting it from external interference.
- Aligns the trust with moral and ethical principles rooted in divinity.
- Shields the trust from fraud by emphasizing its foundational legitimacy.

Role 2: The Trustee (Spirit and Agent)

The Trustee is the spirit of the Sigma Trust, acting as the operational manager and intermediary between the Executor and the Beneficiary. The Trustee's role is dynamic, bridging divine purpose with earthly execution.

Responsibilities of the Trustee:

- Managing trust assets and ensuring their growth and protection.
- Executing the Executor's directives in accordance with the trust's purpose.
- Representing the trust in external dealings, such as contracts and negotiations.
- Acting as the spiritual guide to uphold the trust's moral and ethical values.

Dual Nature of the Trustee:

- **Spirit**: Represents the trust's ethical and spiritual compass, ensuring alignment with its divine mission.

- **Agent**: Acts as the earthly representative, executing tasks and managing operations with precision and efficiency.

Key Advantages of the Trustee Role:

- Ensures the trust's daily operations align with its overarching purpose.
- Maintains a balance between divine authority and earthly practicality.
- Shields the Executor from direct involvement in operational matters, preserving sovereignty.

Role 3: The Beneficiary (Body)

The Beneficiary is the recipient of the Sigma Trust's assets, services, and benefits. This role is fulfilled by the body, symbolizing the human aspect of the trust.

Responsibilities of the Beneficiary:

- Receiving distributions and benefits from the trust as stipulated by its terms.
- Acting in harmony with the trust's spiritual and ethical framework.
- Providing feedback to ensure the trust's operations align with the needs of its intended recipients.

Key Advantages of the Beneficiary Role:

- Ensures that the trust serves its intended purpose of benefiting the body.
- Reflects the material manifestation of the trust's divine and operational principles.
- Creates accountability for the Trustee to act in the Beneficiary's best interests.

Interplay Between Roles

The Sigma Trust's threefold framework creates a
harmonious balance between divine authority,
operational management, and material benefit.

1. **Checks and Balances**: The Executor
   oversees the Trustee, who in turn ensures
   the Beneficiary's needs are met, creating a
   system of accountability.
2. **Legal and Spiritual Integration**: The roles are
   designed to function within legal frameworks
   while honoring the trust's spiritual
   foundations.
3. **Protection and Sovereignty**: The distinct
   separation of roles ensures the trust is
   protected from administrative overreach and
   fraud.

A Practical Example

Imagine the following scenario to illustrate the framework:

- **Executor (God)**: Establishes the Sigma Trust to protect and grow royalties from intellectual property and safeguard assets for future generations.
- **Trustee (Spirit/Agent)**: Manages these royalties and assets, reinvesting them into income-generating opportunities while maintaining ethical practices.
- **Beneficiary (Body)**: Receives the trust's benefits in the form of distributions, services, and protections, while ensuring alignment with the trust's divine purpose.

This structure ensures seamless alignment between spiritual intent, operational execution, and material benefit.

Conclusion

The Executor, Trustee, and Beneficiary roles are central to the Sigma Trust's unique and resilient framework. By intertwining spiritual authority, operational stewardship, and material benefit, the Sigma Trust creates a legally sound and divinely aligned structure.

In the next section, we will explore the complexities of managing these multi-capacity roles and how they interact to create a trust that is sovereign, adaptable, and impervious to external interference.

Section 2: Understanding Multi-Capacity Functions

The Sigma Trust's unique design leverages multi-capacity functions, enabling individuals to embody more than one role within the trust while maintaining legal, ethical, and operational integrity. This concept integrates the spiritual, operational, and material aspects of the trust to create a versatile and resilient framework.

What Are Multi-Capacity Functions?

Multi-capacity functions occur when a single individual or entity fulfills multiple roles within the trust. In the Sigma Trust, this means that one person can simultaneously act as:

1. **Executor (God)** – Establishing divine intent and ultimate authority.
2. **Trustee (Spirit/Agent)** – Managing assets and operations on behalf of the trust.
3. **Beneficiary (Body)** – Receiving benefits and ensuring alignment with the trust's purpose.

While distinct, these capacities work together to achieve the trust's overarching goals. Multi-capacity functions ensure flexibility and continuity, particularly in highly personalized or spiritually aligned trusts like the Sigma Trust.

Benefits of Multi-Capacity Functions

1. **Efficiency**: Streamlines decision-making and execution, as the same individual

understands the trust's purpose and
operational requirements intimately.

2. **Alignment**: Ensures that all roles operate in
   harmony, reducing conflicts of interest.
3. **Control**: Enhances the grantor's ability to
   guide the trust's direction and manage its
   operations.
4. **Sovereignty**: Protects the trust from external
   interference by consolidating control within a
   well-defined legal structure.

Potential Challenges and Solutions

1. **Conflict of Interest**:
   - ○ **Challenge**: Acting in multiple
     capacities may create apparent or
     perceived conflicts.
   - ○ **Solution**: Establish clear legal
     documentation outlining the
     responsibilities and boundaries of

each role. Maintain detailed records to demonstrate impartiality and adherence to fiduciary duties.

2. **Legal Scrutiny**:
   - **Challenge**: Multi-capacity roles may attract heightened scrutiny from administrative agencies or courts.
   - **Solution**: Ensure the trust complies with local laws and regulations. Obtain legal advice to structure the trust in a manner that withstands administrative challenges.

3. **Operational Overload**:
   - **Challenge**: One individual managing multiple roles may lead to inefficiencies or mistakes.
   - **Solution**: Delegate specific administrative tasks to professionals or advisors while retaining ultimate control as the Executor.

Interplay of Roles in Multi-Capacity Functions

1. **Executor and Trustee**:
   The Executor (God) defines the spiritual and foundational purpose of the trust, while the Trustee (Spirit) ensures its practical implementation. These roles complement each other, with the Trustee acting as the hands of the Executor's vision.
2. **Trustee and Beneficiary**:
   The Trustee (Spirit/Agent) must act in the best interests of the Beneficiary (Body). This interplay ensures that the trust's resources are utilized effectively and ethically, balancing operational needs with material benefits.
3. **Executor and Beneficiary**:
   The Executor's (God's) divine intent safeguards the Beneficiary's (Body's) well-being, ensuring that the trust remains aligned with its higher purpose while serving practical needs.

Practical Example of Multi-Capacity Functions

Scenario:
A grantor establishes the Sigma Trust to manage royalties from published works, protect assets, and ensure long-term benefits for their descendants. The grantor assumes multiple roles:

- **Executor**: Declares the trust's intent to promote intellectual growth and spiritual well-being through royalties and donations.
- **Trustee**: Manages the trust's assets, invests in income-generating opportunities, and ensures ethical practices.
- **Beneficiary**: Receives distributions to fund personal projects, living expenses, or charitable endeavors.

Through multi-capacity functions, the grantor maintains control over the trust's vision while ensuring operational efficiency and material benefit.

Legal Safeguards for Multi-Capacity Roles

1. **Clear Documentation**:
   - Establish the distinct roles and responsibilities in the trust deed.
   - Include clauses that address potential conflicts of interest and outline solutions.
2. **Fiduciary Standards**:
   - Adhere to fiduciary duties of loyalty, care, and impartiality when acting as Trustee or Agent.
   - Document all decisions to demonstrate alignment with the trust's purpose.
3. **Third-Party Advisors**:
   - Engage legal, financial, or tax advisors to ensure compliance and mitigate risks.

Conclusion

Understanding and implementing multi-capacity functions allows the Sigma Trust to operate efficiently, ethically, and in alignment with its higher purpose. By clearly defining the interplay between Executor, Trustee, and Beneficiary, the Sigma Trust establishes a framework that is both resilient and adaptable.

In the next section, we will explore how the Sigma Trust integrates protections against administrative overreach and fraud, ensuring its sovereignty and longevity.

Section 3: How Each Role Protects the Trust and Assets

In the Sigma Trust, each role—Executor, Trustee, and Beneficiary—serves not only to manage and distribute assets but also to protect the integrity of the trust and its assets from external threats, legal challenges, and administrative fraud. Each role is strategically designed to act as a safeguard, ensuring the trust's longevity, ethical operations, and adherence to its spiritual, operational, and material goals. This section explores how each role provides vital protection for the trust and its assets.

1. Executor (God) and Protection

The Executor, representing the divine principle (God), is the foundational authority behind the Sigma Trust. This role provides a level of spiritual sovereignty and ethical guidance that is crucial in protecting the trust from external influences, fraud, and unethical practices.

Protection Features of the Executor Role:

- **Sovereign Authority**: The Executor's divine position grants ultimate authority over the trust, shielding it from interference by external agencies, governments, or other third parties. This sovereignty creates a legal and moral defense against challenges, as the trust is grounded in a higher, unassailable purpose.
- **Purpose and Intent**: The Executor's role is to establish and declare the trust's mission, vision, and ethical framework. This spiritual direction ensures that the trust operates with integrity, thus reducing the likelihood of fraud or misuse of assets.
- **Divine Jurisdiction**: The Executor's divine authority can be used to claim exemption from certain legal requirements or administrative procedures that may be exploitative or intrusive.

This helps to shield the trust's assets and operations from unjust taxation or overreach.

- **Immunity from Administrative Control**: By establishing the trust under the Executor's divine guidance, the trust is not subject to the same legal structures that might otherwise govern conventional entities. This helps protect the trust from unwarranted government intervention or other forms of administrative control.

---

2. Trustee (Spirit and Agent) and Protection

The Trustee, as both the spirit and the operational agent, serves as the manager of the trust. This role is essential in ensuring the day-to-day protection and growth of the trust's assets. The Trustee ensures that the trust is managed in accordance with the Executor's divine purpose while also providing a layer of protection through prudent decision-making and operational oversight.

Protection Features of the Trustee Role:

- **Fiduciary Duty**: The Trustee is bound by fiduciary duties of loyalty and care, ensuring that they act in the best interests of the trust, its purpose, and the Beneficiary. By upholding these duties, the Trustee minimizes the risk of mismanagement, fraud, or malfeasance.

- **Asset Management**: As the operational agent of the trust, the Trustee is responsible for the prudent management of assets. This includes diversifying investments, protecting intellectual property (such as copyrights or trademarks), and ensuring that the trust's resources are utilized effectively and in line with its divine purpose.
- **Legal Shielding**: The Trustee's role often involves shielding the trust from legal challenges. By ensuring the trust complies with all relevant legal and tax regulations, the Trustee helps protect the trust from potential legal actions or financial penalties that could deplete its assets.
- **Operational Transparency**: The Trustee provides a clear and transparent record of all decisions and actions taken on behalf of the trust. This transparency helps protect the trust from accusations of negligence or mismanagement, as all actions are documented and align with the trust's established goals.
- **Protection from Fraud**: The Trustee acts as the first line of defense against fraud. This involves ensuring that all assets are properly accounted for, investments are legitimate, and the trust's activities are above board. By having a professional and ethical Trustee, the risk of exploitation or manipulation is minimized.

3. Beneficiary (Body) and Protection

The Beneficiary, representing the body, is the recipient of the trust's benefits. While the Beneficiary is primarily concerned with receiving the fruits of the trust's activities, their role is also crucial in protecting the trust's integrity and ensuring that the trust remains aligned with its purpose.

Protection Features of the Beneficiary Role:

- **Beneficiary Rights**: The Beneficiary holds the right to receive distributions from the trust according to its terms. This right ensures that the trust is accountable to its stated mission and goals, thus preventing the misuse or misdirection of assets.
- **Oversight and Accountability**: As the Beneficiary is the ultimate recipient of the trust's benefits, they provide an additional layer of oversight. The Beneficiary can ensure that the Trustee and Executor are fulfilling their duties correctly and ethically. If necessary, the Beneficiary can hold the Trustee accountable for any failures to act in their best interests.
- **Ensuring Continuity**: The Beneficiary plays a critical role in ensuring that the trust continues to fulfill its purpose. If the Beneficiary is a person or a family, they can establish long-term objectives for the trust's operation and ensure

that it serves future generations in accordance with its foundational principles.

- **Material Protection**: The Beneficiary ensures that the trust's material assets (e.g., royalties, property, or intellectual property) are protected by keeping track of distributions and ensuring that resources are allocated effectively. If the trust is benefiting multiple beneficiaries, this role helps maintain equity in the distribution of resources.
- **Enforcement of Ethical Standards**: The Beneficiary helps enforce the trust's ethical standards by ensuring that the Trustee acts in the spirit of the trust's mission. This provides a safeguard against any potential abuse or deviation from the trust's original intent.

---

4. How the Roles Interact to Protect the Trust and Assets

The interplay between the Executor, Trustee, and Beneficiary creates a comprehensive system of checks and balances, where each role reinforces the other to ensure the trust's protection from external threats and mismanagement.

- **Executor and Trustee**: The Executor, by establishing the divine purpose, guides the

Trustee's operational management. The Trustee, in turn, ensures that the trust's assets are managed according to this divine intent, providing protection from misuse. Together, they form the core legal and spiritual framework of the trust.

- **Trustee and Beneficiary**: The Trustee is responsible for ensuring that the Beneficiary receives the benefits of the trust's operations. The Beneficiary, in turn, holds the Trustee accountable by ensuring that distributions are fair, equitable, and in line with the trust's mission. This creates a layer of protection against exploitation or mismanagement.
- **Executor and Beneficiary**: The Executor ensures that the trust remains aligned with its divine purpose, which ultimately benefits the Beneficiary. By maintaining spiritual and ethical principles, the Executor provides a safeguard against potential exploitation or deviation from the trust's intended goals.

Conclusion

Each role in the Sigma Trust—Executor, Trustee, and Beneficiary—plays a critical part in safeguarding the trust's assets, operations, and integrity. By delineating these roles and ensuring that each one fulfills its specific responsibilities, the Sigma Trust creates a robust framework that offers protection from legal, ethical, and administrative threats. This comprehensive approach ensures that the trust remains resilient, ethical, and focused on its foundational goals.

In the next section, we will explore the legal protections that can be incorporated into the Sigma Trust, further strengthening its ability to withstand challenges and safeguard its assets.

Section 4: Case Studies of Multi-Capacity Implementation

Understanding how the Sigma Trust operates in practice is essential to appreciating the versatility and robustness of its multi-capacity framework. This section presents real-world case studies that illustrate the successful implementation of the multi-capacity roles within the trust. These case studies demonstrate the operational efficiency, asset protection, and legal sovereignty provided by the integration of the Executor, Trustee, and Beneficiary roles in various scenarios.

Case Study 1: Intellectual Property Management in the Sigma Trust

Scenario:
An author establishes the Sigma Trust to manage their intellectual property, including copyrights, trademarks, and royalties from published works. The trust is designed to protect the author's creative works from external interference and ensure that royalties are distributed in a way that aligns with the author's long-term vision.

Roles and Responsibilities:

- **Executor (God)**:
  The Executor, representing the divine principle, sets the purpose of the trust: to ensure that the author's intellectual property is preserved for future generations, promoting creativity and educational growth. The Executor's role is to determine how the royalties should be reinvested, with the ultimate goal of ensuring the works contribute to a greater societal good.
- **Trustee (Spirit/Agent)**:
  The Trustee manages the copyrights and trademarks, ensuring that all legal protections are in place and that any infringements are actively pursued. The Trustee is also responsible for negotiating licensing agreements, ensuring that

the works are used ethically and in accordance
with the Executor's divine purpose. This role
ensures that the intellectual property is generating
revenue and serving the community in line with
the trust's mission.

- **Beneficiary (Body)**:
The Beneficiary, potentially the author's family
or a designated charity, receives royalties
generated from the intellectual property. These
funds are allocated for living expenses,
educational purposes, or reinvested into new
creative projects. The Beneficiary ensures that
the royalties are used for the greater good,
adhering to the ethical guidelines set by the
Executor.

Protection Mechanisms:

- The intellectual property is shielded from
external claims and government control
through the Executor's divine jurisdiction.

- The Trustee ensures all legal defenses are
in place to protect the copyrights from
infringement.

- The Beneficiary ensures that the assets are
used to further the trust's mission and
prevent wasteful spending.

Case Study 2: Real Estate Holdings and Wealth Management

Scenario:
A family creates the Sigma Trust to manage a portfolio of real estate properties and investments. The trust is designed to preserve the family wealth for future generations, minimizing taxes and ensuring that the assets are protected from creditors or potential legal claims.

Roles and Responsibilities:

- **Executor (God)**:
  The Executor's divine intent focuses on preserving the family's wealth, passing it down through generations in a way that honors the family's legacy. The Executor determines the long-term investment strategy and provides guidance on how the properties should be used to fulfill the family's ethical obligations to the community.
- **Trustee (Spirit/Agent)**:
  The Trustee manages the real estate holdings, ensuring that the properties are maintained, rented, or sold in alignment with the Executor's goals. The Trustee handles the day-to-day

operations, including tenant relations, maintenance, and legal matters, and ensures that the portfolio remains profitable and well-protected from potential claims or disputes.

- **Beneficiary (Body)**:
The family members or future generations are the beneficiaries who receive income from the properties. The Beneficiary ensures that the wealth is used for the betterment of the family, including education, health, and charitable giving. They also play a role in ensuring that the wealth is passed down ethically and is not squandered.

Protection Mechanisms:

- The Executor's oversight ensures that the assets are used in a way that is morally sound, reducing the risk of misuse or exploitation.
- The Trustee acts as a legal shield, maintaining the properties and ensuring they are insulated from claims by creditors or legal challenges.
- The Beneficiary ensures that the trust remains focused on preserving wealth for

future generations, using it to create positive impacts in society.

Case Study 3: Charitable Giving and Community Investment

Scenario:
An entrepreneur sets up the Sigma Trust to manage their wealth and direct it toward charitable causes and community projects. The goal is to ensure that the funds are used to support social programs, education, and infrastructure in underserved areas, aligning with the entrepreneur's personal values.

Roles and Responsibilities:

- **Executor (God)**:
  The Executor's role is to define the overarching purpose of the trust, which is to serve the public good. This includes determining which causes and projects will benefit from the trust's assets and ensuring that the charity's work remains aligned with the original intent of giving back to the community.
- **Trustee (Spirit/Agent)**:
  The Trustee oversees the distribution of funds to

approved charities and community projects. The Trustee ensures that all donations are made in accordance with the Executor's divine vision, ensuring transparency, accountability, and ethical allocation of resources. They also manage any investments related to the charitable projects to ensure sustainability and long-term impact.

- **Beneficiary (Body)**:
The Beneficiary, in this case, could be the communities receiving the charitable funds. They ensure that the trust's contributions are used for their intended purposes, such as building schools, funding healthcare, or developing local businesses. The Beneficiary works to ensure that the trust remains relevant and responsive to the needs of the community.

Protection Mechanisms:

- The Executor ensures that the charitable giving aligns with ethical and spiritual values, minimizing the risk of misdirected funds or misuse.
- The Trustee acts as a steward of the trust's resources, ensuring that funds are allocated efficiently and ethically.

- The Beneficiary ensures that the funds reach the intended recipients and have a lasting, positive impact on the community.

Case Study 4: Protecting Personal Assets and Income Streams

Scenario:
An individual with significant personal wealth, including business income, investments, and other assets, establishes the Sigma Trust to protect their assets from legal challenges and to manage their income streams in a tax-efficient manner.

Roles and Responsibilities:

- **Executor (God)**:
  The Executor outlines the long-term vision for the individual's assets, focusing on preserving wealth while minimizing taxes and legal exposure. The Executor's divine guidance ensures that the assets are used for the individual's well-being and for charitable or family purposes in line with ethical values.

- **Trustee (Spirit/Agent):**
  The Trustee is responsible for managing the business income, investments, and other assets. This includes ensuring compliance with tax laws, handling financial transactions, and managing business operations. The Trustee protects the individual's wealth by separating personal assets from the potential risks associated with business activities.
- **Beneficiary (Body):**
  The individual is the primary Beneficiary, receiving distributions from the trust for personal use, including lifestyle maintenance, healthcare, and future planning. The Beneficiary ensures that the assets are used responsibly and in line with the long-term goals set by the Executor.

Protection Mechanisms:

- The Executor's divine intent ensures that the individual's wealth is used in a way that promotes spiritual and material well-being.

- The Trustee manages the assets to shield them from legal claims, creditor actions, or other potential risks, preserving the individual's wealth and ensuring tax efficiency.

- The Beneficiary ensures that distributions are made in accordance with the Executor's guidelines, avoiding wasteful spending or misuse of trust resources.

Conclusion

The case studies presented illustrate how the Sigma Trust's multi-capacity framework functions in various contexts, providing asset protection, tax efficiency, and spiritual alignment. The roles of Executor, Trustee, and Beneficiary work together to safeguard the trust from legal challenges, fraud, and misuse, ensuring that the trust's assets are used ethically and responsibly. By integrating these roles, the Sigma Trust provides a robust and versatile framework for managing and protecting wealth, intellectual property, charitable endeavors, and personal assets.

In the next section, we will explore the legal protections that can be added to the Sigma Trust to further enhance its resilience and ability to withstand challenges from external entities.

Chapter 3: Funding the Sigma Trust

Section 1: Initial Funding: Transferring Assets into the Trust

The process of funding the Sigma Trust is a critical step in ensuring that the trust can achieve its intended purposes. This section explores the various methods for transferring assets into the Sigma Trust, examining how to structure the initial funding to align with the trust's goals of asset protection, tax efficiency, and legal sovereignty.

---

1. Understanding the Role of Funding in the Sigma Trust

Before transferring assets into the Sigma Trust, it's important to understand that the initial funding is what empowers the trust to fulfill its purpose. Assets transferred into the trust are effectively removed from personal ownership and are controlled by the trust, subject to the conditions and stipulations set forth in the trust agreement. This separation from personal ownership is essential for achieving asset protection, tax advantages, and other legal benefits.

Key Concepts:

- **Legal Ownership vs. Beneficial Ownership:** When assets are transferred into the Sigma Trust, legal ownership is held by the trust, but the Beneficiary retains beneficial ownership, meaning they can still use and enjoy the assets in accordance with the trust's terms.

- **Irrevocability**: Once assets are placed into the Sigma Trust, the transfer is permanent. The assets cannot be reclaimed or altered by the grantor unless the trust agreement allows for such changes, reinforcing the irrevocable nature of the trust.

2. Types of Assets that Can Be Transferred into the Sigma Trust

The Sigma Trust can hold a wide range of assets, and choosing the right assets for funding the trust is crucial for meeting its long-term objectives. Common types of assets that can be transferred include:

- **Real Estate**: Property titles can be transferred into the trust, providing protection from personal creditors and ensuring the property is preserved according to the terms of the trust.

- **Financial Assets**: Cash, stocks, bonds, and other investment assets can be transferred into the trust, enabling efficient management of investments and the potential for tax deferral or minimization.
- **Intellectual Property**: Copyrights, trademarks, patents, and other forms of intellectual property can be assigned to the trust. This is a particularly important strategy for creators looking to protect and monetize their intellectual property through royalties or licensing agreements.
- **Business Interests**: Ownership stakes in businesses or other commercial entities can be placed into the trust, ensuring the continuity of business operations and shielding assets from legal liabilities.
- **Personal Property**: Valuable personal property such as jewelry, artwork, or

collectibles can also be transferred into the trust, safeguarding them from external claims and ensuring they pass down according to the trust's terms.

Funding Strategy Example:

- A business owner may transfer the ownership of a corporation into the trust. This allows the business to continue operating under the guidance of the Trustee (the spirit) while ensuring that it is shielded from personal creditors and legal disputes involving the individual. The Beneficiary (the body) will still receive income and benefits from the business, but the assets are protected by the trust.

3. Methods of Transferring Assets into the Sigma Trust

Once the assets are selected for inclusion in the trust, they must be formally transferred to the trust. Each type of asset requires a different method of transfer:

- **Real Estate**:
  Real property is transferred to the trust through a deed of transfer. This legal document must be executed by the current owner (the Grantor) and recorded with the local government. The deed typically states that the property is being transferred to the trust and identifies the trustee as the new legal owner.
- **Financial Accounts**:
  For financial accounts such as bank accounts, brokerage accounts, or retirement accounts, the title of the account must be changed to reflect the trust as the account holder. This may involve submitting forms to the financial institution and may require the establishment of a new account under the trust's name.
- **Intellectual Property**:
  Intellectual property rights are transferred to the trust through an assignment agreement. This document outlines the transfer of ownership of the intellectual property, such as trademarks or copyrights, to the trust. The transfer must be recorded with the appropriate governing bodies

(e.g., the U.S. Patent and Trademark Office for trademarks).

- **Business Interests**:
  Business interests, including shares in a corporation or membership interests in an LLC, are transferred to the trust by changing the ownership on corporate records. This process may involve the issuance of new stock certificates or updating the membership records to reflect the trust as the owner.
- **Personal Property**:
  Personal property can be transferred into the trust through a bill of sale or an assignment document. For high-value items, such as art or jewelry, a formal appraisal and written agreement may be required to establish the transfer of ownership.

4. Addressing Tax Implications When Funding the Sigma Trust

Transferring assets into the Sigma Trust can have significant tax implications, which must be carefully managed to ensure compliance and optimize tax efficiency. Here are the key considerations:

- **Gift Tax**:
  In some jurisdictions, transferring assets into a trust can be considered a gift, potentially

triggering gift tax liability. The IRS, for example, allows individuals to transfer a certain amount of wealth without incurring gift tax. However, large transfers may trigger taxes, so it's important to ensure that the transfers are made within legal limits or structured to avoid these taxes.

- **Capital Gains Tax**:
When transferring certain types of assets, such as real estate or stocks, capital gains tax may apply if the assets have appreciated in value. However, irrevocable trusts can sometimes be structured to minimize the impact of capital gains taxes by allowing assets to grow tax-deferred within the trust.

- **Income Tax Considerations**:
Depending on how the Sigma Trust is structured, the income generated from trust assets may be taxed at the trust level or passed through to the Beneficiary. Understanding the income tax implications is essential for maintaining the trust's tax efficiency.

Tax Strategy Example:

- If the Grantor transfers a highly appreciated asset, such as a family home, into the trust, the trust may not be immediately liable for capital gains taxes if structured correctly. Over time, the asset's value may increase, but because it is held by the trust, the gains can be shielded from taxation or passed through to the Beneficiary in a tax-efficient manner.

---

5. Potential Challenges and How to Overcome Them

While transferring assets into the Sigma Trust is a strategic move, there are several potential challenges that may arise during the process. These challenges include:

- **Complexity of Asset Transfers**:
  Transferring certain assets, especially those with complex legal or financial structures, can be complicated and time-consuming. Working with attorneys, accountants, and financial professionals is essential to ensure that the transfer is done correctly and efficiently.
- **Resistance from Third Parties**:
  Third parties, such as financial institutions or business partners, may resist the transfer of assets into the trust, especially if they have a vested interest in maintaining control over the assets. Clear communication and legal documentation are key to overcoming these obstacles.

- **Valuation of Assets**:
  In some cases, assets may need to be professionally appraised to determine their fair market value at the time of transfer. This is especially important for personal property, intellectual property, and business interests.

Conclusion

The process of funding the Sigma Trust is an essential step in ensuring that the trust operates smoothly and achieves its intended purposes of asset protection, tax efficiency, and legal sovereignty. By carefully selecting and transferring assets into the trust, individuals can create a legal framework that shields their wealth from external claims, reduces tax liabilities, and preserves their assets for future generations. As with any complex legal structure, working with professionals and adhering to the proper procedures is critical to the success of the trust's funding process.

In the next section, we will explore the ongoing management and operation of the Sigma Trust, focusing on how to ensure the trust remains aligned with its original purpose while adapting to changing circumstances.

Section 2: Continuous Contributions:

Donations, Royalties, and Income Streams

A key feature of the Sigma Trust is its capacity to
continually grow and sustain itself through ongoing
contributions. Unlike traditional trusts, which may rely
solely on an initial funding, the Sigma Trust is designed
to accept continuous infusions of assets in the form of
donations, royalties, and other income streams. This
section will explore how these contributions function
within the Sigma Trust and contribute to its long-term
sustainability and protection of assets.

---

1. Understanding the Role of Continuous

Contributions

In the context of the Sigma Trust, contributions are not
limited to the initial transfer of assets but can include
ongoing donations and income that support the trust's
purposes. These contributions help ensure that the trust
remains financially robust, allowing it to fulfill its
mission of asset protection, sovereignty, and tax
efficiency. Donations, royalties, and income streams also
provide a steady flow of resources that can be used for
the trust's intended goals, whether it's paying for

operational costs, supporting beneficiaries, or furthering the growth of assets.

Key Considerations:

- **Asset Accumulation**: Continuous contributions enable the Sigma Trust to accumulate wealth and assets over time, which can be reinvested into the trust to strengthen its financial foundation.
- **Financial Independence**: These ongoing contributions give the trust greater autonomy and reduce reliance on external sources of funding, enabling it to remain independent from government or institutional control.
- **Sustainability**: By accepting regular donations, royalties, and income, the Sigma Trust can ensure its sustainability even as external economic conditions fluctuate.

2. Donations: Structuring Gifts to the Sigma Trust

One of the primary ways to fund the Sigma Trust is through donations. Donations to the trust can come in various forms, including cash, assets, or property. The key benefit of donations is that they provide an infusion of resources that are immediately placed under the trust's control, while the donor retains no further claim to the assets once they are transferred.

Donation Types and Benefits:

- **Cash Donations**: Straightforward and easy to manage, cash donations can quickly be added to the trust's account, providing immediate liquidity for the trust.
- **Asset Donations**: Physical assets such as real estate, intellectual property, or business interests can be donated to the trust. These donations protect the assets from potential future claims while allowing the trust to benefit from their use or income.

- **Stock and Securities Donations**: Donating stocks or securities to the trust provides both immediate and long-term benefits, including potential tax advantages depending on the asset's value and tax treatment.

Tax Benefits of Donations:

Donating assets to an irrevocable trust, such as the Sigma Trust, can offer significant tax benefits, including:

- **Charitable Donation Deductions**: If the trust is structured to allow for charitable purposes, donations may qualify for charitable deductions under applicable tax laws, reducing the donor's taxable estate.
- **Gift Tax Exemption**: Donations to an irrevocable trust may be exempt from gift taxes up to certain limits, depending on the jurisdiction and the value of the donation.

3. Royalties: A Steady Income Stream for the Trust

For creators, intellectual property owners, and business stakeholders, royalties can serve as a consistent source of income for the Sigma Trust. These payments arise from the use, sale, or licensing of assets such as trademarks, copyrights, patents, and other intellectual property held by the trust.

Royalties and the Sigma Trust:

- **Intellectual Property Licensing**: The Sigma Trust can hold intellectual property rights (such as copyrights, trademarks, and patents), which it can license to third parties. In return, the trust receives royalties, which are then used for the benefit of the trust's beneficiaries.
- **Revenue from Creative Works**: Authors, musicians, inventors, and artists can assign their royalties to the Sigma Trust, ensuring

that future income from their creative works is preserved and protected under the trust.

- **Royalty Agreements**: To formalize the process, the trust can enter into royalty agreements with companies, individuals, or organizations interested in using the intellectual property. These agreements can be tailored to provide the trust with a regular stream of income.

Case Study Example:

An author may assign the rights to their published works to the Sigma Trust. The trust can then license those rights to publishers, earning royalties from book sales, digital rights, or other licensing agreements. This provides a long-term revenue stream for the trust while the author's intellectual property is legally protected and managed by the trustee.

4. Income Streams: Investments and Business Activities

Another key aspect of sustaining the Sigma Trust is through the generation of income via investments or business operations. The trust can engage in a wide range of income-generating activities, which help the trust grow and maintain its operations.

Types of Income Streams:

- **Investment Income:** The trust can invest in stocks, bonds, real estate, or other financial instruments. The income generated from these investments can be used to support the trust's objectives, while the assets themselves remain protected within the trust.
- **Rental Income:** If the trust owns real estate, rental income from properties can be a consistent source of funding. The trust may own both residential and commercial properties, which generate income through leasing or rental agreements.

- **Business Operations**: The Sigma Trust can operate or own businesses, and the income generated from those operations is directed back into the trust. Whether through ownership of a small business or investments in larger ventures, this income supports the trust's activities.

Example of Investment Strategy:

If the trust has been funded with cash or securities, the trustee may decide to invest those funds in a diversified portfolio of stocks, bonds, and real estate. The earnings from dividends, interest, and capital gains are then reinvested back into the trust, continuing to grow its assets over time.

5. Structuring Contributions to Minimize Risk and Maximize Protection

As with any financial structure, it is essential to properly manage and structure the continuous contributions to ensure they align with the trust's legal and financial goals. The goal is to maximize the benefits of these contributions while minimizing potential risks, such as fraud or mismanagement.

Strategies for Safe Contributions:

- **Diversification of Income Streams**: By ensuring that the trust benefits from multiple income sources—such as royalties, investments, and business operations—the trust can minimize risk and ensure long-term sustainability.

- **Regular Documentation and Reporting**: Keeping thorough records of all contributions, whether donations or royalties, helps maintain transparency and protects the trust from legal challenges. This documentation also ensures that tax filings are accurate and compliant with the law.

- **Third-Party Agreements**: Any agreements related to royalties or business operations should be drafted with legal oversight to protect the trust's interests and ensure that third parties adhere to the terms.

6. Addressing Legal and Tax Considerations for Continuous Contributions

While continuous contributions can significantly benefit the Sigma Trust, it is essential to understand the legal and tax implications of these ongoing additions. Here are the key factors to consider:

- **Taxation on Royalties**: Royalties earned by the trust are generally subject to income tax, but there may be opportunities to structure the trust in ways that minimize these taxes, such as by utilizing tax-exempt provisions or deductions related to charitable purposes.
- **Gift Tax on Ongoing Donations**: If ongoing donations exceed certain thresholds, the donor may be subject to gift taxes. Strategic

planning is essential to ensure that
donations remain within tax-exempt limits.
- **Trustee's Role in Managing Contributions**:
The Trustee must ensure that all
contributions are handled in a way that
complies with the terms of the trust and with
relevant tax laws. This includes overseeing
the distribution of royalties and ensuring that
donations are properly documented.

Conclusion

Continuous contributions, whether in the form of
donations, royalties, or income streams, are essential for
maintaining the financial health and sovereignty of the
Sigma Trust. These contributions enable the trust to
grow and protect assets over time, while ensuring that it
remains independent and sustainable. By carefully
managing these contributions and aligning them with the
trust's goals, the Sigma Trust can provide long-term
protection, tax benefits, and legal advantages for its
beneficiaries. In the next section, we will explore the
management and operation of the trust, focusing on how

the assets and income are distributed and how the trust
remains aligned with its mission.

Section 3: Strategic Asset Placement:

Intellectual Property, Investments, and More

Strategic asset placement is a cornerstone of the Sigma
Trust's design. By placing assets in carefully selected
categories, such as intellectual property, investments,
real estate, and more, the trust can maximize both
protection and growth potential. This section will delve
into the optimal methods for structuring and placing
assets within the Sigma Trust to achieve long-term
sustainability, tax benefits, and legal protection, all while
maintaining the trust's independence and integrity.

1. Intellectual Property: A Core Asset for the Sigma Trust

Intellectual property (IP) is one of the most powerful and valuable types of assets that can be held within the Sigma Trust. IP, including copyrights, trademarks, patents, and trade secrets, represents creative, innovative, or commercial value and can provide substantial ongoing revenue through royalties, licensing, and other arrangements.

Key Forms of Intellectual Property for the Trust:

- **Copyrights**: These protect original works of authorship, including literary works, music, art, software, and more. The trust can hold copyrights to creative works and earn income from licensing them to third parties.
- **Trademarks**: Trademarks protect distinctive marks, logos, names, or other identifiers used in commerce. The trust can register and protect trademarks that it owns, ensuring their exclusivity and protecting them from infringement.

- **Patents**: A patent grants exclusive rights to an invention or process. The trust can own patents for inventions it creates or acquires, generating income through licensing or sales.
- **Trade Secrets**: These include confidential business information, formulas, or processes. The trust can protect and manage trade secrets to ensure their value remains intact and undisclosed.

Strategic Use of Intellectual Property:

- **Revenue Generation**: Intellectual property can be licensed or sold to generate income for the trust. Royalties from copyrighted works, licensing fees from trademarks, and earnings from patents can provide a consistent income stream.
- **Branding and Marketability**: The trust can leverage its trademarks to build brand recognition, marketing partnerships, and

business ventures. A well-managed trademark portfolio can enhance the trust's commercial value.

- **Protection from Legal Claims**: By holding intellectual property within the trust, the assets are protected from creditors and lawsuits, providing a shield from legal claims against the trust's beneficiaries.

---

2. Investments: Diversifying the Trust's Portfolio

Investing assets wisely is a fundamental strategy for the Sigma Trust to ensure long-term financial growth. A diversified investment portfolio helps mitigate risks while maximizing potential returns. The Sigma Trust can hold various investment vehicles, from traditional stocks and bonds to alternative investments like real estate, private equity, and business interests.

Types of Investments for the Trust:

- **Stocks and Bonds**: The trust can invest in publicly traded stocks, bonds, and mutual funds to generate income and appreciate in value. Equity investments in companies can provide dividends, while bonds offer predictable returns through interest payments.

- **Real Estate**: Real estate is a tangible asset that provides both potential appreciation and steady cash flow through rental income. The Sigma Trust can acquire residential, commercial, or industrial properties, diversifying its holdings while generating a stable income stream.

- **Private Equity and Venture Capital**: The trust can participate in private equity or venture capital investments, where it funds startups or established companies in exchange for equity ownership. These investments can offer high returns but also come with higher risks.

- **Commodities and Alternative Investments**: Commodities like gold, silver, oil, and agricultural products can serve as a hedge against inflation and market volatility. Additionally, alternative investments like hedge funds, cryptocurrencies, and collectibles may also be considered for diversification.

Investment Strategy:

- **Risk Management**: A diversified portfolio spreads risk across various asset classes, ensuring that the trust's overall value is less susceptible to market fluctuations.
- **Tax Efficiency**: Investments held within the trust may be structured to maximize tax efficiency, reducing capital gains taxes, and taking advantage of any available tax deferrals or exemptions.

- **Income Generation**: Investments such as bonds, dividend-paying stocks, or rental properties provide steady income streams, ensuring that the trust remains self-sustaining and can continue to support its mission.

---

3. Real Estate: Building Tangible Wealth for the Trust

Real estate is an excellent way to provide both immediate income and long-term capital appreciation to the Sigma Trust. Whether through the ownership of residential, commercial, or industrial properties, real estate investments can offer multiple benefits, including tax advantages, asset protection, and revenue generation.

Real Estate Strategies for the Sigma Trust:

- **Rental Properties**: The Sigma Trust can invest in residential or commercial rental properties, which generate consistent rental income. These properties may be leased to tenants, providing cash flow while appreciating in value over time.

- **Development Projects**: The trust can invest in property development, purchasing land or underdeveloped property and improving it for resale or long-term investment.
- **Property Flipping**: For higher-risk strategies, the trust could engage in property flipping, purchasing distressed properties, renovating them, and selling them for a profit.
- **Land Ownership**: Owning land provides long-term appreciation potential, along with opportunities for leasing, farming, or resource extraction.

Tax Benefits of Real Estate Investments:

- **Depreciation**: Real estate properties can be depreciated over time, providing tax deductions for the trust.

- **Capital Gains Tax**: If the property appreciates in value and is sold for a profit, the trust may benefit from favorable capital gains tax rates, particularly if the property is held for over a year.
- **1031 Exchange**: The trust may also be able to take advantage of a 1031 exchange, which allows it to defer taxes on the gain from the sale of one property by reinvesting the proceeds into another like-kind property.

---

4. Business Interests: Owning and Operating Businesses

The Sigma Trust can also hold and operate businesses, either as an active participant or by holding ownership stakes in various ventures. This strategy enables the trust to directly influence its growth, generate income, and further its mission while managing risks effectively.

Business Ventures for the Sigma Trust:

- **Entrepreneurial Activities**: The trust can create or invest in businesses, ranging from startups to established companies. By holding equity in these businesses, the trust benefits from profits, dividends, and eventual sales or mergers.
- **Franchising**: The trust can invest in or operate franchises, which often come with a proven business model and an established brand, reducing the risk associated with new ventures.
- **Income-Generating Assets**: If the trust owns a business, it can create additional income streams, such as providing services, products, or licensing intellectual property.

Benefits of Business Ownership within the Trust:

- **Control over Income**: By directly participating in business activities, the trust can ensure that it generates a reliable and potentially lucrative income stream.

- **Tax Advantages**: Business income can be structured in ways that maximize tax benefits, including deductions for business expenses, depreciation of assets, and credits for research and development activities.
- **Risk Mitigation**: By operating within the trust, business assets and liabilities are insulated from personal claims or external creditors, providing an added layer of protection.

5. Structuring Asset Placement to Optimize Trust's Goals

The strategic placement of assets within the Sigma Trust should align with the trust's long-term goals, including asset protection, financial growth, and independence. A few key principles include:

- **Separation of Personal and Trust Assets**: The trust should not hold assets that are personally owned by individuals in a way that could expose the trust to personal liabilities. Assets should be clearly transferred to the trust to avoid confusion or conflict.
- **Diversification**: By diversifying the types of assets held within the trust—across intellectual property, investments, real estate, and business interests—the Sigma Trust can reduce risk and maximize growth potential.
- **Legal Compliance**: All assets must be placed in accordance with applicable laws and regulations to ensure that the trust remains in good standing and maintains its protections against claims from external entities.

Conclusion

Strategic asset placement is critical for achieving the Sigma Trust's objectives of asset protection, tax efficiency, and financial independence. By effectively managing intellectual property, investments, real estate, and business interests, the trust can create a diversified and resilient financial foundation. Each asset class serves to both protect the trust's holdings from external threats and generate consistent revenue streams, ensuring long-term success for the trust and its beneficiaries. In the next section, we will examine the operational management of the trust, focusing on how the assets are managed and distributed.

Section 4: Transferring Social Security Benefits Without Waiting

In this section, we explore the process of transferring Social Security benefits into the Sigma Trust, ensuring that the trust gains control over these funds without the typical delays and bureaucratic hurdles. The goal is to integrate Social Security benefits into the trust's structure immediately, securing these funds while maintaining full protection from administrative agencies and fraud risks.

1. Understanding Social Security Benefits and Trusts

Social Security benefits are typically provided by government agencies and are often assigned to individuals through a Social Security number (SSN). These benefits can include retirement income, disability payments, and survivor benefits. However, the challenge lies in transferring and protecting these benefits while keeping them within the structure of an irrevocable trust, such as the Sigma Trust.

Social Security benefits are often considered "government-administered" funds, which makes them difficult to directly place into a trust without certain legal protections. The main concern is ensuring that the funds transferred into the trust are not subject to bureaucratic control, fraud, or misuse by administrative agencies.

Key Considerations for Social Security Benefit Transfer:

- **Government Restrictions**: Social Security benefits are typically intended for the direct benefit of individuals, making it difficult to assign these benefits to a third-party entity, such as a trust. This requires strategic planning and an understanding of administrative procedures.

- **Trust as a Beneficiary**: One potential avenue is to designate the trust as the beneficiary of the Social Security benefits, rather than transferring the benefits directly into the trust itself.
- **Legal Safeguards**: It's essential to ensure that all transfers are compliant with Social Security laws and regulations, particularly in light of restrictions that may prevent direct assignment of these funds to the trust.

2. Structuring the Trust to Receive Social Security Benefits

To transfer Social Security benefits to the Sigma Trust without waiting, we must carefully structure the trust and its provisions. While it may not be possible to transfer funds directly into the trust immediately, there are ways to ensure that the trust receives the benefits in an effective manner.

Designating the Trust as the Payee:

One effective strategy is to designate the trust as the payee for Social Security benefits. This can be done by submitting a formal request to the Social Security Administration (SSA) to have the trust receive the payments on behalf of the individual, under certain conditions. This process allows the trust to manage the funds directly, while still receiving Social Security benefits as intended.

Using the Trust's Tax Identification Number (TIN):

By applying for a tax identification number (TIN) for the trust, the SSA can potentially issue payments directly to the trust, using this unique identifier. This helps maintain the integrity of the trust and ensures that payments are made in alignment with its structure, without the funds being considered part of an individual's personal assets.

Incorporating a Spendthrift Clause:

A spendthrift clause in the Sigma Trust can be used to restrict the trust's beneficiaries from using Social Security funds inappropriately, ensuring that the funds are only used for the intended purpose. This legal mechanism offers additional protection, shielding the funds from creditors or misuse.

---

3. Legal Mechanisms for Immediate Control

Although it may not be immediately possible to transfer Social Security benefits into the trust itself, certain legal mechanisms can be used to gain control over the benefits and protect them from fraud or administrative abuse.

Cestui Que Vie Trust Transfer:

One potential method is using a Cestui Que Vie trust structure, where the Social Security benefits are effectively transferred under the legal control of the Sigma Trust. The Cestui Que Vie trust can be structured to include provisions for the trust to receive income on behalf of the individual, even if it is not the direct recipient of the Social Security payments.

Power of Attorney (POA):

A power of attorney can be utilized to allow the Sigma Trust's designated agents to manage the individual's Social Security benefits on their behalf. This grants the trust control over the decision-making process regarding the funds, allowing the trust to manage the payments and

ensure proper allocation to protect the individual and
their assets.

Financial Proxy Arrangements:

In some cases, a financial proxy arrangement can be
made, where a trusted representative (or the trustee) is
appointed to handle the Social Security payments for the
individual. This ensures that the trust, or a representative
of the trust, manages and disburses the funds according
to the established terms of the trust.

4. Addressing Administrative and Legal

Barriers

The most significant challenge in transferring Social
Security benefits to a trust is navigating the complex
bureaucracy of governmental agencies. Social Security
payments are typically tied to an individual's SSN, and
there are strict regulations in place that prevent the direct
transfer of these benefits into third-party accounts.

Overcoming Governmental Restrictions:

While the government may initially resist or place
limitations on transferring Social Security benefits

directly into the trust, leveraging legal precedents, such as the principles of sovereign immunity and trust law, can provide a framework for petitioning these agencies. Legal actions, like filing for a formal review or challenging any undue restrictions, can help in securing the transfer.

Legal Documentation and Proof:

To address potential objections from administrative agencies, ensure that all documentation required by the SSA and other government entities is thoroughly prepared and submitted. This includes proving that the trust is irrevocable, demonstrating that the beneficiary's needs will be properly met by the trust, and providing evidence of the legitimacy of the trust's purposes.

Litigation as a Last Resort:

If efforts to transfer Social Security benefits into the Sigma Trust are obstructed by administrative agencies, litigation can be considered as a last resort. A well-prepared legal challenge to the Social Security Administration's refusal to transfer benefits can compel the agency to comply with the law or settle the matter through court.

5. Protecting the Trust from Fraud and Administrative Overreach

Given the increasing risks of fraud and administrative overreach, it's essential to ensure that the Sigma Trust is protected at all stages of the transfer process.

Fraud Prevention Mechanisms:

The Sigma Trust should include strict fraud protection clauses, ensuring that all assets transferred into the trust, including Social Security benefits, are safeguarded from external tampering or misuse. This includes periodic audits of the trust's activities, as well as a transparent tracking system to monitor the flow of funds and ensure compliance with trust terms.

Maintaining Autonomy from Administrative Agencies:

To prevent administrative agencies from gaining control over the Sigma Trust's assets, it's critical to establish clauses that limit the ability of government bodies to interfere with the trust's operations. This includes setting up legal protections against unwarranted garnishments, levies, or claims.

Conclusion

Transferring Social Security benefits to the Sigma Trust
without waiting for bureaucratic approval is a
challenging but achievable goal. Through strategic
structuring, such as designating the trust as the payee,
applying for a TIN, and using power of attorney or
financial proxies, the Sigma Trust can take control over
these benefits. Legal mechanisms, like Cestui Que Vie
trusts and spendthrift clauses, add further protection and
ensure the trust remains a secure and autonomous entity.
With careful planning and execution, the Sigma Trust
can safeguard Social Security benefits while protecting
its assets from fraud, administrative interference, and
external threats.

Chapter 4: Asset Protection Strategies

Section 1: Shielding the Trust from Administrative Agencies

In this section, we will explore effective strategies to protect the Sigma Trust from potential interference, oversight, and manipulation by administrative agencies. Given the growing influence of government bodies and the risk of arbitrary legal actions, understanding how to shield the trust is critical to preserving its autonomy, integrity, and its ability to protect assets.

1. Legal Foundations of Asset Protection

The foundation of any effective asset protection strategy lies in the understanding of trust law, sovereign immunity, and the limits of administrative power. The Sigma Trust, by its very design as an irrevocable trust, creates a distinct legal entity that operates independently of personal assets, shielding its contents from creditors and legal liabilities. However, the growing reach of administrative agencies necessitates advanced protection mechanisms.

Key Legal Principles:

- **Irrevocability of the Trust**: By ensuring that the trust is irrevocable, it becomes much harder for external agencies to influence or seize assets once they are transferred into the trust. The irrevocable nature of the Sigma Trust ensures that the grantor (you) no longer have control over the assets, creating a protective shield.

- **Sovereign Immunity**: The concept of sovereign immunity may apply to some legal structures, allowing certain entities to avoid interference by government bodies. By structuring the Sigma Trust in a way that establishes the principal as a sovereign entity, it can be positioned as immune from administrative control.

2. Structuring the Trust to Limit Administrative Overreach

One of the primary ways to shield the Sigma Trust from administrative agencies is through strategic structuring. This includes creating provisions and clauses that limit or restrict the ability of these agencies to intervene in the operations or assets of the trust.

Spendthrift Clauses:

A spendthrift clause restricts the trust beneficiaries' ability to access or assign their rights to trust assets. This protection also shields the assets from creditors, including government agencies that may attempt to claim the trust's assets for any outstanding obligations or penalties. By incorporating a spendthrift clause, the Sigma Trust ensures that its assets remain beyond the reach of most creditors.

Discretionary Distribution Powers:

Giving the trustee discretionary powers regarding the distribution of assets allows for a layer of protection against administrative actions. If the trustee has full discretion over when and how assets are distributed, the trust becomes more resistant to intervention. Administrative agencies may find it difficult to claim specific assets since they are not guaranteed to be available for beneficiaries.

Irrevocable Terms and Protections:

The irrevocable nature of the Sigma Trust, combined with carefully crafted terms, ensures that the assets remain secure. Administrative agencies typically cannot alter or challenge the terms of an irrevocable trust, preventing external interference. The trust's assets must be fully protected, and the beneficiaries' rights are defined and secured in accordance with the terms of the trust.

3. Legal Protections Against Garnishment and Seizure

Asset protection is not limited to preventing fraud but also to ensuring that trust assets are not subject to garnishment, seizure, or other forms of administrative encumbrance. Given the growing trend of aggressive actions by government bodies in seizing assets, protecting the trust from such tactics is paramount.

Garnishment Protections:

One of the most important tools in protecting trust assets is to establish clauses that explicitly prohibit garnishment or seizure by external authorities, including tax agencies and government entities. The Sigma Trust can include a legal provision that protects its assets from garnishment, including those that arise from government claims, tax liens, or judgments.

Severability Clauses:

A severability clause ensures that if one part of the trust is found to be unenforceable, the rest of the trust remains intact. This is particularly important in the event that an administrative agency attempts to challenge certain provisions of the trust. The severability clause prevents a legal challenge to invalidate the entire trust based on one issue.

Protections Against Writs of Attachment:

Writs of attachment allow government agencies to seize property or assets for debts. By incorporating language that explicitly restricts the use of such writs on trust assets, the Sigma Trust can effectively guard itself from asset seizure by administrative agencies.

4. Strategic Use of Private and Public Entities for Protection

The Sigma Trust can also shield itself by utilizing private and public entities that offer legal protections against governmental overreach. These include non-profit organizations, private foundations, or other legal structures that serve as intermediaries or protectors.

Establishing a Protector Role:

A protector is an independent third party who is not a beneficiary or trustee, but who has certain oversight powers over the trust. The protector's role is to ensure that the terms of the trust are followed and that the interests of the beneficiaries are protected, especially in the case of external interference. By appointing a trusted protector, the Sigma Trust creates an additional layer of protection from administrative agencies that may attempt to exert control.

Utilizing International Trust Structures:

In some cases, international trusts or foreign jurisdictions may offer more robust protections against U.S. administrative agencies. Certain foreign jurisdictions provide heightened confidentiality and asset protection laws that can shield the trust from U.S. government claims. Though complicated and requiring due diligence, establishing an international trust component can create a secure environment for the trust's assets.

Collaborating with Non-Profit Entities:

Non-profit organizations, such as those established under Section 501(c)(3) of the Internal Revenue Code, may provide an additional layer of protection. These entities benefit from certain tax-exempt status and can act as intermediaries between the Sigma Trust and external administrative agencies, shielding the trust's assets from claims. The collaboration of the Sigma Trust with such organizations could provide strategic legal protections and greater autonomy.

5. Minimizing Risks of Administrative Interference

To minimize the risk of administrative agencies seeking to undermine or manipulate the Sigma Trust, it's crucial to build defenses into the structure of the trust. These defenses help ensure that the trust maintains control over its assets, even in the face of governmental pressure.

Audit and Transparency Clauses:

An audit clause can be added to the trust to ensure transparency and accountability without allowing outside agencies to gain control over trust funds. While transparency is critical for legal compliance, it is important to prevent unnecessary exposure that could attract administrative scrutiny. A balanced approach can ensure that the trust operates with integrity while protecting its privacy.

Non-Discriminatory Terms and Purposes:

By structuring the trust with non-discriminatory, non-political, and non-religious terms, it is less likely to attract unwanted scrutiny from government bodies. Administrative agencies may be less inclined to challenge a trust that operates in the public interest or provides services without engaging in contentious political or social matters.

Continual Legal Review and Updates:

Since laws and regulations are subject to change, it's important to periodically review the trust's terms and its protections. Regular legal consultations and updates to the trust's structure will ensure that it remains in compliance with any new laws and continues to protect its assets from administrative agencies effectively.

Conclusion

Shielding the Sigma Trust from administrative agencies requires a multifaceted approach that combines strong legal principles, strategic structuring, and ongoing vigilance. By leveraging irrevocable terms, spendthrift clauses, discretionary distribution powers, and legal safeguards such as severability clauses and garnishment protections, the Sigma Trust can preserve its integrity and independence. Additionally, by appointing protectors, utilizing international structures, and collaborating with non-profit entities, the trust can build further layers of defense against administrative overreach. Finally, regular legal reviews and updates ensure the trust remains secure and effective in its mission to protect assets and provide long-term stability for its beneficiaries.

Section 2: Protecting Intellectual Property:

Trademarks and Copyrights

In this section, we will explore how the Sigma Trust can effectively protect its intellectual property (IP), specifically trademarks and copyrights. Intellectual property is one of the most valuable assets held by creators, businesses, and individuals alike. Proper protection of IP ensures its exclusive use and prevents unauthorized exploitation. For the Sigma Trust, IP protection serves as a critical component in preserving the trust's wealth, reputation, and ability to generate income.

1. Defining Intellectual Property:

Trademarks and Copyrights

Before delving into protection strategies, it's essential to understand what constitutes intellectual property and the legal mechanisms that protect it.

Trademarks:

A trademark is a distinctive sign, symbol, logo, or word that represents a business or product. It grants the owner exclusive rights to use that mark in commerce, preventing others from using it without permission. Trademarks help establish brand identity and customer loyalty and can become some of the most valuable assets of a business or individual.

- **Purpose of Trademarks**: To distinguish goods or services from others in the market and to safeguard the reputation associated with the mark.
- **Sigma Trust Considerations**: The Sigma Trust may hold trademarks for the name, logos, or branding associated with its operations, such as the "Sigma Trust" name or any intellectual property related to its function and services.

Copyrights:

Copyright is a form of protection granted to the creators of original works, including literary, artistic, musical, and other intellectual works. Copyright grants the creator exclusive rights to reproduce, distribute, perform, and display the work.

- **Purpose of Copyrights**: To protect the creative expression and originality of works and ensure that the creator has control over how the work is used.

- **Sigma Trust Considerations**: The Sigma Trust may own copyrights to works such as books, music, artworks, software, and other creative content that generates income through royalties and licensing.

2. Registering Trademarks and Copyrights: Establishing Ownership

In order for the Sigma Trust to legally protect its intellectual property, the trademarks and copyrights must be properly registered with the relevant authorities. This establishes legal ownership and provides enforcement rights if infringement occurs.

Trademark Registration:

To protect the Sigma Trust's name, logo, and other branding elements, it must be registered with the United States Patent and Trademark Office (USPTO) or relevant international bodies. Registration provides several benefits:

- **Exclusive Rights**: Registered trademarks give the Sigma Trust exclusive use of the mark in relation to the goods or services it provides.
- **Legal Presumption of Ownership**: Registration provides a legal presumption that the trust owns the trademark and has the right to use it in commerce.
- **Infringement Protection**: If a third party infringes upon the trademark, the Sigma Trust can take legal action to stop the infringement and seek damages.
- **Nationwide Protection**: Registration offers nationwide protection, preventing others from using a similar mark in a way that could confuse consumers.

Copyright Registration:

Similarly, to protect the Sigma Trust's original works, it should register its copyrights with the U.S. Copyright Office or the relevant copyright authority in other jurisdictions. Registration allows the trust to:

- **Establish Ownership**: Copyright registration provides proof of ownership and the date the work was created, which is essential for protecting the work from infringement.
- **Enforce Rights**: A registered copyright allows the Sigma Trust to take legal action against those who infringe upon its works, seeking remedies such as statutory damages and attorney's fees.
- **International Protection**: Copyright protection is extended internationally through treaties like the Berne Convention, ensuring that the Sigma Trust's works are protected in other countries.

3. Enforcing IP Rights: Protection from Infringement

Once trademarks and copyrights are registered, it is essential for the Sigma Trust to actively monitor and enforce its intellectual property rights. Protecting IP from infringement and unauthorized use is a critical function for maintaining the value of these assets.

Trademark Infringement Protection:

- **Monitoring Use**: The Sigma Trust should regularly monitor the marketplace and digital platforms to ensure no one is using its trademarks without permission. This can be done through IP watch services or by keeping an eye on online platforms and competitors.
- **Cease and Desist Letters**: If infringement occurs, the first step is usually to send a cease and desist letter to the infringing party, demanding they stop using the trademark. This letter is a formal request to halt the unauthorized use and can serve as the first step in legal action.
- **Legal Action**: If the infringement continues or cannot be resolved amicably, the Sigma Trust may pursue legal action. This can

include filing a lawsuit for trademark infringement in federal court and seeking damages for any losses incurred as a result of the infringement.

Copyright Infringement Protection:

- **Monitoring Copyright Usage**: The Sigma Trust should monitor the use of its copyrighted works across various media platforms, including websites, social media, and other public domains.
- **Digital Millennium Copyright Act (DMCA)**: If a copyrighted work is infringed online, the Sigma Trust can issue a DMCA takedown notice to the platform hosting the infringing content. This legal tool forces platforms to remove or block access to infringing material.
- **Enforcement Through Litigation**: In cases where informal cease and desist methods fail, the Sigma Trust may initiate litigation for

copyright infringement, seeking statutory damages, actual damages, and attorney's fees.

4. Licensing and Royalties: Maximizing the Value of IP

Intellectual property rights, once protected, can serve as a source of ongoing revenue through licensing and royalties. By licensing its IP to other entities, the Sigma Trust can generate income streams, all of which are deposited into the trust for asset protection and future growth.

Licensing IP Rights:

The Sigma Trust can license its trademarks and copyrights to third parties, granting them the right to use the IP for a specified period and under defined conditions. Licensing agreements should clearly outline the terms of use, compensation, and any restrictions to ensure the trust maintains control over the IP's use.

- **Exclusive vs. Non-Exclusive Licensing**: The trust can grant exclusive licenses (where only one licensee can use the IP) or non-exclusive licenses (where multiple parties can use the IP). Exclusive licensing can generate higher fees but limits the trust's ability to use the IP in other markets.

Royalties:

Royalties represent ongoing payments made by licensees to the Sigma Trust in exchange for the right to use its IP. These payments can come in various forms, such as:

- **Fixed Fees**: A one-time fee for the right to use the IP.
- **Ongoing Royalties**: Periodic payments based on sales or use of the licensed IP. This can provide a steady stream of income for the Sigma Trust.
- **Performance-based Royalties**: Royalties tied to the performance or sales volume of products or services incorporating the IP.

5. Safeguarding IP for Future Generations

Protecting intellectual property is not just about
immediate enforcement and revenue generation; it's also
about ensuring that these assets are preserved for the
long term, benefiting future generations.

Transferring IP into the Sigma Trust:

Intellectual property should be transferred into the Sigma
Trust for optimal protection. Once transferred, the trust
holds legal ownership of the IP, and the revenue
generated from it flows back into the trust. This ensures
the long-term preservation of the IP and its associated
income streams, while also protecting the assets from
potential creditors or administrative claims.

Estate Planning for IP:

The Sigma Trust can ensure that IP assets are passed on
to future generations in a tax-efficient manner by
incorporating the intellectual property into the overall
estate plan. The trust can specify how the IP will be
managed, licensed, and transferred, ensuring that the
assets continue to generate revenue and remain protected
from external threats.

Conclusion

Protecting intellectual property is a critical aspect of the Sigma Trust's strategy for wealth preservation and asset growth. By registering trademarks and copyrights, the Sigma Trust can secure exclusive rights to its valuable creations. Active enforcement through monitoring, cease and desist letters, and legal action ensures that these rights are upheld, while licensing and royalties provide valuable income streams. By transferring IP into the trust and implementing estate planning strategies, the Sigma Trust can safeguard its intellectual property for future generations, ensuring its long-term value and protection from administrative agencies or creditors.

Section 3: Legal Safeguards Against Fraudulent Claims

In the context of the Sigma Trust, ensuring that the trust's assets and operations remain protected from fraudulent claims is paramount. Fraudulent claims can arise from a variety of sources, including creditors, administrative agencies, or even individuals seeking to exploit the trust's resources or misappropriate its assets. This section will discuss the key legal safeguards that can be employed to prevent and protect against fraudulent claims, ensuring the integrity of the Sigma Trust and the security of its assets.

---

1. Proper Trust Documentation and Execution

The foundation of any successful defense against fraudulent claims begins with the proper creation, documentation, and execution of the Sigma Trust. Trusts that are poorly drafted or lack clarity in their terms may be more vulnerable to challenges or fraudulent claims.

Clear and Precise Trust Agreements:

The trust document must clearly outline the intentions, duties, and responsibilities of all parties involved (e.g., the trustee, beneficiaries, agents). Ambiguity in the document may leave room for exploitation or fraudulent manipulation by parties seeking to undermine the trust. Therefore, the Sigma Trust's document should:

- **Clearly Define Roles and Capacities**: It should specify who the principal, trustee, agent, and beneficiaries are, and the distinct

roles each party plays in the operation of the
trust.

- **Outlining Powers and Limitations**: It should
  include explicit provisions regarding the
  powers granted to the trustee and other key
  parties. This will prevent unauthorized
  actions or claims that could threaten the
  trust's assets.
- **Documenting Asset Transfers**: All assets that
  are transferred into the trust should be well-
  documented. This includes proper legal
  instruments such as deeds, contracts, or title
  transfers, ensuring that there are clear
  records of asset ownership by the trust.

---

2. Trust Protector and Independent Oversight

A trust protector is an independent party or entity
appointed to oversee the administration of the trust and
ensure that its terms are followed as intended. This

individual or entity acts as a safeguard against potential fraudulent actions by the trustee or other parties involved in the trust.

Role of the Trust Protector:

- **Oversight of Trustee Actions**: The trust protector can oversee the trustee's actions, ensuring that the trustee is not engaging in self-dealing or making decisions that benefit themselves at the expense of the trust or its beneficiaries.
- **Dispute Resolution**: In the event of conflicts or disputes over the trust's administration or asset distribution, the trust protector can step in to mediate and ensure that the trust's terms are adhered to.
- **Termination or Modification of Trust**: A trust protector can be granted the power to modify or even terminate the trust in cases where the trust's purpose is being compromised or to prevent harm to the trust due to fraudulent actions.

This layer of oversight helps create an additional level of security, making it more difficult for fraudulent claims to succeed.

---

3. Asset Segregation and Protection

One of the key objectives of the Sigma Trust is asset protection. To effectively shield the trust's assets from fraudulent claims, the assets must be carefully segregated and structured in a way that makes them difficult for outside parties to access.

Segregating Trust Assets from Personal Assets:

- **No Co-mingling**: The trust should avoid co-mingling its assets with personal assets. By keeping trust assets in separate accounts and titles, the trust ensures that its assets are legally distinct and protected from claims on the individual or other entities.
- **Use of Trust Entities**: In certain cases, the trust may use other legal entities (e.g., limited liability companies or special purpose

entities) to further shield its assets from fraudulent claims. These entities can serve as holding companies for certain assets, reducing the risk of exposure to legal challenges.

Insurance Protections:

- **Liability Insurance**: The Sigma Trust can purchase liability insurance policies to protect against legal claims, including those that may arise from fraudulent claims or malicious actions. This insurance can cover legal defense costs, settlements, or damages that may be incurred in the event of a lawsuit.
- **Asset Protection Insurance**: In addition to liability insurance, the trust can take out asset protection insurance to cover the loss or theft of valuable assets, providing an additional layer of security against claims.

4. Fraud Prevention Clauses in the Trust Document

To further protect the trust, the Sigma Trust should include specific provisions designed to prevent fraudulent claims and protect the integrity of the trust. These clauses act as proactive measures that can be invoked in the event of an attempt to defraud the trust.

Fraudulent Conveyance Clause:

A fraudulent conveyance occurs when assets are transferred to the trust with the intent to defraud creditors or avoid legal responsibilities. The trust should include provisions stating that any transfers made to the trust are legitimate, and that the trust will not be used to shield assets from legitimate claims or liabilities.

- **Documentation and Evidence Requirements**: To combat fraudulent conveyance, the trust document can require that any transfer of assets into the trust be fully documented and supported by legitimate and verifiable sources (e.g., tax returns, income statements).

- **Presumption of Fraud**: If a claim of fraudulent conveyance is made, the trust could include a clause that requires the claimant to prove the fraudulent intent by clear and convincing evidence, making it more difficult for fraudulent claims to succeed.

No Contest Clause:

A no contest clause (also known as an "in terrorem" clause) is a provision that discourages beneficiaries or other interested parties from challenging the validity of the trust. If someone contests the trust and loses, they risk losing their benefits or inheritance under the trust.

- **Deterrence of Baseless Claims**: This clause serves to discourage beneficiaries from making frivolous or fraudulent claims, knowing that if their claims are deemed to be without merit, they may forfeit their right to any benefit from the trust.

Incorporating a Dispute Resolution Mechanism:

The Sigma Trust can include provisions that require any
disputes regarding the trust to be resolved through
arbitration or mediation rather than through costly and
time-consuming litigation. By avoiding the courts, the
trust reduces the exposure to fraudulent claims and
ensures that any challenges to the trust are handled in a
controlled and legal manner.

5. Monitoring and Auditing

Active monitoring and auditing of the trust's activities
can help to identify and respond to potential fraudulent
claims early, minimizing the risk of harm to the trust's
assets.

Annual Audits:

The Sigma Trust should undergo regular audits
performed by an independent third party. These audits
will examine the trust's financial records, asset transfers,
and other critical activities to ensure compliance with the
terms of the trust and to identify any signs of fraudulent
activity.

Regular Legal Reviews:

Legal counsel should conduct regular reviews of the
trust's operations to ensure that all actions taken by the
trustee, agents, and other parties involved are in
compliance with the law and the terms of the trust. These
reviews help identify any weaknesses in the trust's
structure that may make it vulnerable to fraudulent
claims.

Conclusion

Fraudulent claims pose a significant threat to the security
and stability of the Sigma Trust. By implementing strong
legal safeguards—including clear and precise
documentation, the appointment of a trust protector,
asset segregation, fraud prevention clauses, and ongoing
monitoring—the Sigma Trust can ensure that its assets
are protected and its operations remain secure from
fraudulent claims. These protections are essential for
maintaining the integrity of the trust, ensuring that the
trust's assets and income streams remain safeguarded for
future generations.

Section 4: Building a Firewall Against Creditors and Third-Party Claims

In the context of the Sigma Trust, building a robust firewall to protect the trust's assets from creditors and third-party claims is a critical component of its asset protection strategy. The Sigma Trust's structure, combined with effective legal safeguards, ensures that its assets remain insulated from the reach of creditors, governmental agencies, and others who may seek to seize or claim those assets. This section explores how to establish and strengthen this firewall, focusing on key strategies that prevent access to the trust's resources, preserve the integrity of the trust, and maintain the autonomy of its beneficiaries.

---

1. Legal Separation: Distinguishing Trust Assets from Personal Assets

One of the most effective ways to protect trust assets from creditors and third-party claims is to ensure that there is a clear legal separation between the assets held within the Sigma Trust and the personal assets of the trustee or beneficiaries.

Trust as a Separate Legal Entity:

- **Distinct Ownership**: By ensuring that the assets of the Sigma Trust are held in the name of the trust, and not the trustee or beneficiaries personally, it establishes a legal boundary that creditors cannot easily breach. This separation prevents creditors from accessing the trust's assets to satisfy personal debts of the trustee, beneficiaries, or other related parties.

- **Proper Titling of Assets**: Assets such as real estate, intellectual property, and investments must be titled in the name of the trust. This prevents any ambiguity regarding ownership, ensuring that third parties cannot claim those assets as theirs in the event of a personal financial dispute.

Avoiding Co-Mingling of Funds:

- **Separate Accounts**: The trust should maintain its own bank accounts, separate from any personal accounts used by the trustee or beneficiaries. This reinforces the distinction between personal finances and trust assets, minimizing the risk of third parties accessing funds that are legally designated for the trust.

2. Spendthrift Provisions: Protecting Against Creditors' Claims

A spendthrift provision is a clause within the Sigma Trust that restricts creditors' ability to seize trust assets to satisfy the debts of the beneficiaries. This provision ensures that the assets are protected from claims made by creditors, as long as the beneficiary is not personally liable for those debts.

Protecting Beneficiaries' Interests:

- **No Creditor Access to Benefits**: A spendthrift clause prohibits creditors from accessing the assets or income of the trust for purposes such as debt collection, alimony, or other financial obligations. This ensures that the trust's assets remain secure and are only used for the benefit of the trust's designated purposes.

- **Asset Protection for Beneficiaries**: This protection ensures that if a beneficiary faces financial difficulties or litigation, the trust assets are not at risk. In the event of bankruptcy or personal financial crises, the beneficiaries' interests in the trust are shielded from creditors seeking to seize those assets.

Limited Exceptions to Spendthrift Protections:

While spendthrift provisions are powerful tools, there are certain exceptions to their enforceability, depending on the jurisdiction. For example:

- **Child Support or Alimony**: Some jurisdictions allow creditors to access trust assets in the case of child support or alimony obligations. However, with proper legal structuring, these risks can be minimized through careful design of the trust.
- **Fraudulent Transfers**: If the transfer of assets to the trust is deemed to have been made with fraudulent intent (i.e., to avoid existing or potential creditors), a court may override the spendthrift clause.

3. The Role of Irrevocability: Immutability as a Shield

One of the core features of the Sigma Trust is its irrevocability, which serves as a powerful shield against creditors and third-party claims. The irrevocable nature of the trust ensures that the trust assets cannot be easily accessed, modified, or dissolved by the settlor (creator of the trust) or any other party.

Preventing Alterations or Revocation:

- **No Revocation or Modification**: The irrevocable nature of the trust means that once assets are transferred into it, they are no longer under the direct control of the settlor or the trustee. This prevents creditors from demanding the return or alteration of assets, ensuring that the trust's resources remain protected.
- **Protection from Settlor's Creditors**: Because the settlor relinquishes control of the assets once they are placed in the trust, those

assets are shielded from claims made against the settlor's personal creditors. This makes it more difficult for creditors to attack the assets under the guise of "altering" or "revoking" the trust.

Immutability of Trust Terms:

- The irrevocable trust also serves to prevent any subsequent changes to the trust's provisions that could weaken its asset protection structure. Creditors cannot pressure the trustee or beneficiaries into changing the trust terms to allow for access to its assets.

4. Asset Protection Trusts (APTs): Offshore or Domestic Structuring

In addition to the standard provisions within the Sigma Trust, one option for enhanced protection is the use of asset protection trusts (APTs). These specialized trusts are designed specifically to safeguard assets from creditors and third-party claims, both domestically and internationally.

Domestic Asset Protection Trusts (DAPTs):

Some U.S. states have enacted laws allowing for the creation of Domestic Asset Protection Trusts (DAPTs), which provide a higher level of protection for assets placed within the trust. These trusts can offer significant protection against creditors, provided that the trust complies with state-specific legal requirements.

- **Strong State Law Protections**: States such as Nevada, South Dakota, and Alaska have some of the strongest DAPT laws in the U.S., making them ideal jurisdictions for establishing a Sigma Trust with additional creditor protection.
- **Limited Self-Settled Trusts**: In some cases, the Sigma Trust can be structured as a self-settled asset protection trust, where the settlor is also a beneficiary. In these cases, the settlor may still retain certain benefits

from the trust, but creditors may find it difficult to claim those assets.

Offshore Asset Protection Trusts (OAPTs):

For even greater protection, assets within the Sigma Trust may be transferred to an Offshore Asset Protection Trust (OAPT) established in a jurisdiction with strong protections against creditors, such as the Cook Islands, Nevis, or the Cayman Islands. These jurisdictions offer:

- **Severe Barriers to Creditor Claims**: Offshore jurisdictions often have laws that severely limit the ability of creditors to access assets held within these trusts. They typically require that the creditor prove fraud or intent to defraud in order to gain access to the assets.
- **Enhanced Confidentiality**: Offshore trusts generally provide a higher degree of confidentiality regarding the identity of the settlor, beneficiaries, and trust assets, which adds an additional layer of protection against third-party claims.

5. Fraudulent Conveyance and Transfer Protection

To further protect the Sigma Trust from third-party claims, particularly in cases where creditors attempt to challenge the legitimacy of asset transfers, the trust must be structured to avoid fraudulent conveyance.

Documenting the Legitimacy of Transfers:

- **Recordkeeping**: Every asset transfer into the trust should be properly documented with clear and verifiable records showing that the assets were transferred in accordance with the legal requirements and were not made with the intent to defraud creditors.
- **Third-Party Appraisals**: In the case of significant asset transfers (e.g., real estate, intellectual property), having third-party appraisers validate the value and legitimacy of the assets being transferred can further

protect the trust against claims of fraudulent
conveyance.

Conclusion

Building a firewall against creditors and third-party
claims is a multifaceted process that involves clear legal
separation of trust assets, the inclusion of spendthrift
provisions, the irrevocability of the trust, and strategic
use of asset protection strategies such as Domestic or
Offshore Asset Protection Trusts. By carefully
implementing these protections, the Sigma Trust can
ensure that its assets remain insulated from external
threats, preserving the trust's integrity and safeguarding
its resources for the benefit of its intended beneficiaries.
These strategies collectively create a robust defense
against any attempts by creditors or third parties to
access or claim the trust's assets.

Chapter 5: Tax Strategies and Legal Compliance

Section 1: The Sigma Trust and Tax Exemption

One of the most compelling aspects of an irrevocable trust, especially in the case of the Sigma Trust, is its potential for tax exemption. By carefully structuring the trust, it can be positioned to minimize or eliminate certain tax liabilities, particularly in relation to income and estate taxes. This section explores how the Sigma Trust can achieve tax-exempt status, the types of taxes it can be exempt from, and the necessary compliance measures that must be taken to ensure that the trust operates within the bounds of the law.

1. Understanding Tax Exemption for Irrevocable Trusts

An irrevocable trust, by nature, is treated as a separate legal entity for tax purposes. As a result, it is required to file its own tax returns and is subject to different tax rules than a living individual. However, with the proper structure, it is possible to create a trust that qualifies for tax exemption, particularly if it is used for specific charitable, religious, or public purposes.

Tax-Exempt Organizations (Section 501(c)(3) Status)

- **Nonprofit and Charitable Purposes**: If the Sigma Trust is established with a charitable or religious purpose, it can apply for Section 501(c)(3) status under the Internal Revenue Code. This designation is granted to organizations that are operated exclusively for charitable, religious, educational, or scientific purposes.

- **Eligibility Criteria**: To qualify for 501(c)(3) status, the trust must demonstrate that its activities are exclusively for exempt purposes. This includes providing charitable services or supporting religious activities. The trust must also ensure that no part of its net earnings inure to the benefit of any private individual or shareholder.
- **Tax Exemption Benefits**: Once granted 501(c)(3) status, the trust will be exempt from federal income taxes on its earnings. Additionally, donations made to the trust may be tax-deductible for the donors, incentivizing contributions to the trust's activities.

Establishing a Religious Trust for Exemption

If the Sigma Trust is designed to serve a religious purpose, it may be eligible for tax-exempt status without needing to apply for 501(c)(3) status. Religious organizations and their trusts are often automatically granted tax-exempt status under the IRS rules.

- **No Formal Application Required**: Many religious organizations are automatically recognized as tax-exempt entities under the Internal Revenue Code, as long as their activities are consistent with religious practices and beliefs.
- **Key Requirements**: To maintain tax-exempt status, the trust must avoid engaging in commercial activities unrelated to its religious purpose. It must also ensure that no private inurement occurs, meaning that no funds are directed toward the personal benefit of the trustees, members, or any individual.

2. Tax Treatment of the Sigma Trust

The tax treatment of the Sigma Trust depends on its specific structure and purpose. A key factor in tax exemption is whether the trust is classified as a **grantor trust** or a **non-grantor trust**.

Grantor Trust: The Settlor Retains Control

In a grantor trust, the settlor (creator of the trust) retains certain powers or interests in the trust, resulting in the settlor being responsible for reporting the trust's income on their personal tax return.

- **Tax Responsibility**: If the Sigma Trust is established as a grantor trust, the settlor (or "grantor") is responsible for paying income taxes on the trust's earnings, as the trust's income is typically passed through to them.
- **Strategic Use of Grantor Trusts**: This structure allows the settlor to retain some control over the trust, but it is subject to specific tax rules that could impact the trust's ability to be exempt from taxes.

Non-Grantor Trust: Separate Tax Entity

Alternatively, the Sigma Trust may be structured as a **non-grantor trust**, where the trust is considered a separate tax entity. This type of trust is taxed on its own income, and the beneficiaries are taxed on the distributions they receive.

- **Tax Filings**: Non-grantor trusts are required to file their own tax returns (IRS Form 1041) and are subject to income taxes on the income the trust generates. The beneficiaries will report distributions as taxable income.
- **Potential for Tax Exemption**: If the Sigma Trust is organized for charitable purposes and qualifies as a 501(c)(3) entity or otherwise operates exclusively for tax-exempt purposes, it can avoid paying income taxes on the trust's earnings.

3. Structuring the Sigma Trust for Optimal Tax Efficiency

To optimize the tax benefits of the Sigma Trust, it is essential to focus on its structure and the nature of its assets. Key strategies include:

Income-Producing Assets

- **Investments and Royalties**: The trust can hold income-producing assets such as royalties, patents, trademarks, or investments in stocks, bonds, and real estate. By ensuring that the assets generate income for the trust, it is possible to create a steady stream of revenue that can be reinvested or distributed for its purposes.
- **Tax-Deferred Growth**: Certain types of income-generating assets, such as retirement accounts, may provide the trust with tax-deferred growth. The Sigma Trust can be structured to hold these assets in a manner that reduces its immediate tax liability while growing its assets over time.

Strategic Tax Planning for Beneficiaries

- **Distributions to Beneficiaries**: Distributions to beneficiaries can be made in a way that minimizes the tax burden on both the trust and its beneficiaries. For example, distributing income to beneficiaries who are in lower tax brackets can reduce the overall tax liability.

- **Income Splitting**: A strategy known as income splitting involves distributing income to multiple beneficiaries in lower tax brackets. This can lower the overall effective tax rate on the income generated by the trust's assets.

Using Trust Assets for Charitable Purposes

- **Charitable Contributions**: The Sigma Trust can engage in charitable giving by donating portions of its income or assets to 501(c)(3) organizations. These donations are tax-deductible, which helps reduce the trust's taxable income.
- **Creating Charitable Trusts**: For long-term tax benefits, the Sigma Trust can set up a

charitable remainder trust (CRT) or charitable lead trust (CLT) to distribute income or principal to a charity while providing tax benefits to the trust and its beneficiaries.

---

4. Compliance with Tax Laws and Reporting Requirements

While tax exemption is a powerful tool, it is crucial for the Sigma Trust to comply with all relevant tax laws and regulations to avoid potential penalties or the loss of its tax-exempt status.

Filing Requirements and Deadlines

- **Annual Tax Filings**: Even though the trust may be tax-exempt, it must still comply with federal, state, and local tax filing requirements. This includes submitting IRS Form 990 (for 501(c)(3) organizations) or

IRS Form 1041 for non-grantor trusts, and ensuring that all income and expenditures are properly documented.

- **Transparency and Accountability**: To maintain its tax-exempt status, the trust must be transparent in its financial activities. This includes maintaining accurate records of all assets, income, and distributions. The IRS and state agencies may audit the trust to verify compliance.

Avoiding Unrelated Business Income Tax (UBIT)

- **UBIT Considerations**: If the Sigma Trust engages in business activities unrelated to its tax-exempt purpose (e.g., generating income through commercial ventures), it could be subject to Unrelated Business Income Tax (UBIT). To avoid this, the trust must ensure that its activities are closely aligned with its exempt purposes and avoid engaging in activities that might trigger UBIT.

- **Risk Management**: If the trust decides to engage in any for-profit ventures, careful planning is required to ensure that the activities do not jeopardize its tax-exempt status.

Conclusion

Tax exemption for the Sigma Trust offers significant advantages, including the ability to shield assets from tax liability, maximize income growth, and protect the trust's resources for long-term benefit. By carefully structuring the trust as a charitable, religious, or nonprofit entity, and implementing strategies to comply with tax laws, the trust can achieve optimal tax efficiency while preserving its assets. Regular compliance with filing requirements and adherence to tax laws are essential to maintaining the trust's tax-exempt status and ensuring its longevity. Through these strategies, the Sigma Trust can serve as both a powerful financial vehicle and a tool for asset protection, aligning with its broader mission and goals.

Section 2: Navigating Tax Laws and Reporting Requirements

Navigating the complex landscape of tax laws and reporting requirements is essential to ensuring the Sigma Trust operates smoothly and maintains its status as a tax-exempt entity. This section will cover the various tax laws that apply to the Sigma Trust, the specific reporting requirements necessary for compliance, and the best practices for ensuring the trust meets all obligations while minimizing its tax burden.

1. Understanding the Trust's Tax Classification

One of the first steps in navigating tax laws for the Sigma Trust is understanding its classification under the Internal Revenue Code (IRC). Trusts can be classified as either **grantor trusts** or **non-grantor trusts**, and the tax treatment will depend on this classification.

Grantor Trusts

In a **grantor trust**, the creator (or "grantor") retains certain powers or control over the trust, such as the ability to revoke it or amend its terms. This type of trust is not considered a separate tax entity; instead, all income generated by the trust is attributed directly to the grantor, and the grantor is responsible for reporting the income on their personal tax return.

- **Tax Responsibility**: The income from the trust will be taxed to the grantor at the applicable individual tax rates.
- **Filing Requirements**: Grantor trusts are generally not required to file a separate tax return. Instead, the grantor includes the trust's income on their personal return using IRS Form 1040 and Schedule E.

Non-Grantor Trusts

A **non-grantor trust** is considered a separate legal entity for tax purposes. It is responsible for paying taxes on any income generated by the trust, and the trust itself files a separate tax return. The beneficiaries will be taxed on distributions they receive from the trust.

- **Tax Responsibility**: The trust itself is responsible for paying taxes on any income it generates, such as interest, dividends, and capital gains. The beneficiaries are responsible for paying taxes on any income they receive from the trust, such as distributions or benefits.

- **Filing Requirements**: Non-grantor trusts must file IRS Form 1041, "U.S. Income Tax Return for Estates and Trusts," to report their income and expenses. The trust must also issue Schedule K-1 to beneficiaries, detailing the income distributed to them.

Tax-Exempt Status for Charitable and Religious Trusts

If the Sigma Trust qualifies as a **charitable or religious trust** under Section 501(c)(3) of the IRC, it may be exempt from paying income taxes. This status is granted when the trust's activities are exclusively charitable, religious, or educational.

- **Application for Tax-Exempt Status**: To obtain tax-exempt status, the trust must file IRS Form 1023 (Application for Recognition of

Exemption) or IRS Form 1024 (Application for Exemption Under Section 501(a)).

- **Ongoing Reporting**: Once granted tax-exempt status, the trust must file an annual information return, IRS Form 990, to report its financial activities. The form is a key tool for ensuring transparency and accountability in the trust's operations.

2. Filing Requirements for Tax-Exempt Trusts

Even if the Sigma Trust is granted tax-exempt status, it is still required to adhere to specific filing requirements to maintain that status. Failure to comply with reporting obligations can result in penalties or the revocation of tax-exempt status. Below are the key filings and deadlines the Sigma Trust must be aware of:

Form 990: Return of Organization Exempt from

Income Tax

For tax-exempt trusts, IRS Form 990 is the primary form for reporting financial activity. This form provides the IRS with detailed information about the trust's income, expenditures, and activities.

- **Annual Filing Requirement**: The trust must file Form 990 annually, even if no taxes are due. This filing includes income and revenue, expenditures, grants, and compensation paid to officers, directors, and trustees.
- **Transparency**: The trust must disclose the compensation for key individuals and any conflicts of interest. Form 990 serves as a public record, allowing the IRS and the public to review how the trust is managing its financial resources.
- **Small Organizations**: Some smaller tax-exempt organizations, depending on their gross receipts, may be eligible to file a

simplified version of Form 990, such as Form 990-EZ or the 990-N (e-Postcard).

Form 1041: U.S. Income Tax Return for Estates and Trusts

If the Sigma Trust is a non-grantor trust, it must file IRS Form 1041 to report income, deductions, gains, and losses. This form is required if the trust earns more than $600 in gross income or has any taxable income during the year.

- **Filing Deadline**: Form 1041 is due on the 15th day of the 4th month after the close of the trust's fiscal year (e.g., April 15th if the fiscal year ends December 31st). An automatic 5-month extension is available by filing IRS Form 7004.
- **Trust Income**: The form must include all income the trust has earned, such as interest, dividends, royalties, or business income. The trust will also report any deductions, such as administrative expenses

or charitable contributions, which may reduce the trust's taxable income.

Schedule K-1: Beneficiary's Share of Income, Deductions, and Credits

Non-grantor trusts are required to issue a Schedule K-1 to each beneficiary. This form reports the income distributions made to each beneficiary and is used by beneficiaries to report their share of the trust's income on their individual tax returns.

- **Reportable Items**: Schedule K-1 details the income distributed to the beneficiary, including ordinary income, capital gains, dividends, and interest. It also reports the beneficiary's share of deductions or credits.
- **Filing with Beneficiary's Tax Return**: Beneficiaries use Schedule K-1 to complete their individual tax returns (Form 1040) and pay taxes on the income distributed to them.

3. Ensuring Compliance with Tax Laws

Complying with tax laws requires consistent attention to detail and thorough record-keeping. The following strategies will help ensure the Sigma Trust remains in good standing with tax authorities:

Maintain Accurate Financial Records

- **Track Income and Expenses**: Keep detailed records of all income received by the trust, including royalties, investment income, and donations. Similarly, track all expenses, including administrative costs, legal fees, and charitable contributions.
- **Document Contributions and Distributions**: Record all donations to the trust and distributions to beneficiaries, ensuring that these actions are fully documented for tax purposes.

- **Legal Counsel**: Work with a legal advisor experienced in trust law to ensure that the Sigma Trust is structured correctly and in compliance with state and federal laws. This will help avoid costly legal issues or challenges to the trust's status.
- **Tax Advisors**: A tax professional who understands the intricacies of trust taxation can help navigate the complexities of reporting and ensure that the trust complies with all tax laws. This includes optimizing the trust's tax position and minimizing liabilities where possible.

Monitor Changes in Tax Laws

- **Stay Informed**: Tax laws can change over time, particularly for trusts and tax-exempt organizations. Regularly review IRS publications and consult with legal or tax

advisors to stay up-to-date on any changes
that may affect the trust's status.

- **Adjust Trust Operations**: If changes to tax
  laws affect the trust's eligibility for tax
  exemption or alter its filing requirements,
  take immediate action to modify the trust's
  operations and ensure continued
  compliance.

4. Avoiding Common Pitfalls

There are several pitfalls that could jeopardize the trust's
tax-exempt status or lead to penalties. Avoiding these
common mistakes is essential to the Sigma Trust's long-
term success.

Failure to File on Time

- **Penalties for Late Filings**: Failing to file Form
  990, Form 1041, or Schedule K-1 on time
  can result in significant penalties. To avoid
  this, ensure that all deadlines are met, and if

necessary, request extensions in a timely manner.

Unrelated Business Income

- **Risk of Losing Tax-Exempt Status**: If the Sigma Trust engages in business activities that are unrelated to its exempt purpose (e.g., commercial ventures), the trust could become liable for unrelated business income tax (UBIT). Avoid these activities unless they are clearly aligned with the trust's exempt goals.

Private Inurement

- **Compliance with No Inurement Rule**: The trust must ensure that no portion of its net earnings benefits private individuals, including trustees or grantors. If private inurement occurs, the trust could lose its tax-exempt status.

Conclusion

Navigating tax laws and reporting requirements is critical to the successful operation of the Sigma Trust. By understanding the tax classification, ensuring timely and accurate filings, and adhering to tax laws, the Sigma Trust can maintain its tax-exempt status, protect its assets, and fulfill its mission. It is essential for the trust to maintain rigorous compliance with federal, state, and local tax requirements while adopting strategies that optimize tax efficiency and minimize liabilities.

Section 3: Tax Efficiency Through Trust Management

Tax efficiency is one of the most important aspects of managing a trust, especially for a complex structure like the Sigma Trust. Proper management of the trust's assets, income, and operations can significantly reduce the overall tax burden, maximizing the benefits to the trust's beneficiaries while maintaining compliance with tax laws. This section will explore key strategies for achieving tax efficiency through trust management, focusing on asset allocation, income distribution, tax-deferred growth, and minimizing taxable events.

1. The Role of Asset Allocation in Tax Efficiency

Effective asset allocation is crucial for tax efficiency, as different asset types are taxed in various ways. By strategically managing the types of assets held within the Sigma Trust, it is possible to minimize tax liabilities and optimize returns.

Diversifying Across Asset Classes

The Sigma Trust can benefit from a diversified portfolio of assets, including:

- **Equities**: Stocks and other equity-based investments often appreciate in value over time, but they may be subject to capital gains taxes upon sale. To optimize tax efficiency, the trust can focus on long-term holdings that qualify for favorable long-term capital gains tax rates.

- **Bonds**: Fixed-income assets such as bonds can offer steady returns, but interest income from bonds is typically taxed at ordinary income rates. Tax-exempt bonds, such as municipal bonds, may be a more tax-efficient alternative, as the interest they generate is often exempt from federal income tax.
- **Real Estate**: Real estate can generate both income and appreciation. Investment properties within the trust may provide tax benefits, including deductions for depreciation. However, the sale of real estate may trigger capital gains taxes unless structured correctly (e.g., through a 1031 exchange).
- **Intellectual Property**: Since the Sigma Trust is designed to manage intellectual property (e.g., trademarks, copyrights), this asset class offers potential for royalty income. Tax efficiency can be achieved by ensuring that these royalties are treated as passive

income rather than active business income, which could subject the trust to higher tax rates.

Tax-Deferred Investments

Some investment types allow income to grow tax-deferred, meaning taxes are not paid until the income is realized (e.g., when the asset is sold). Common examples include:

- **Retirement Accounts**: If the Sigma Trust invests in retirement accounts like IRAs or 401(k)s, it can benefit from tax-deferred growth. These accounts allow assets to appreciate without being taxed until withdrawals are made, often when the beneficiary is in a lower tax bracket.
- **Life Insurance**: Certain life insurance policies allow the trust to accumulate wealth on a tax-deferred basis, and in some cases, provide tax-free benefits to beneficiaries upon the insured's death. Utilizing life

insurance as part of the trust can provide
both tax efficiency and protection for heirs.

By allocating assets across a diverse range of investment vehicles, the Sigma Trust can minimize the tax burden while growing its portfolio over time.

2. Income Distribution: Managing Taxable Events

One of the primary ways to achieve tax efficiency in a trust is through effective income distribution strategies. How and when income is distributed to the trust's beneficiaries can significantly impact the overall tax liability of the trust and its beneficiaries.

Distributing Income to Beneficiaries

In non-grantor trusts, income that is distributed to beneficiaries is generally taxable to them rather than the trust. By distributing income strategically, the trust can reduce its own tax liability and potentially shift income to beneficiaries who are in lower tax brackets.

- **Timing of Distributions**: Distributing income in years when beneficiaries are in lower tax brackets can help reduce the overall tax burden. The trust can also consider making distributions in the form of assets that have appreciated in value (e.g., stocks) to minimize taxable income.
- **Discretionary vs. Mandatory Distributions**: Some trusts allow for discretionary distributions, where the trustee has the flexibility to decide when and how much income to distribute. This flexibility allows the trust to adapt to changing circumstances and manage taxable events more effectively.
- **Beneficiary Tax Brackets**: If the trust has multiple beneficiaries in different tax brackets, distributing income to those in the lowest tax brackets can help reduce the overall tax liability. For example, if one beneficiary is in a 10% tax bracket and another is in a 37% tax bracket, it may be

more tax-efficient to allocate a larger share of income to the lower-bracket beneficiary.

Minimizing Income Through Charitable Contributions

The Sigma Trust can also achieve tax efficiency through charitable contributions. If the trust has a charitable purpose, it can contribute a portion of its income to qualified charitable organizations and potentially benefit from deductions. By making these donations, the trust can reduce its taxable income, which can result in a lower overall tax burden.

- **Charitable Remainder Trusts**: The Sigma Trust could consider using a charitable remainder trust (CRT) as part of its structure. A CRT allows the trust to donate assets to a charity while retaining the right to income from those assets for a specified period. This strategy provides immediate tax deductions for charitable contributions while allowing the trust to continue receiving income.

3. Tax-Deferred Growth: Strategies for Minimizing Taxable Events

Tax-deferred growth allows the Sigma Trust to grow its assets without incurring tax liabilities until the assets are realized. Several strategies can be employed to maximize tax-deferred growth within the trust:

Investing in Tax-Advantaged Accounts

As mentioned earlier, tax-advantaged accounts such as IRAs and 401(k)s offer tax-deferred growth. If the Sigma Trust holds investments in these accounts, the income generated by these assets will not be subject to taxes until they are withdrawn. This allows the trust to grow its investments without worrying about paying taxes on them in the short term.

- **Self-Directed IRAs**: The trust can use a self-directed IRA to invest in a wider variety of assets, including real estate, private equity, and other non-traditional investments. The growth from these investments can be deferred until distributions are made, providing a tax-efficient way to build wealth.

- **Tax-Deferred Annuities**: Another option for tax-deferred growth is purchasing tax-deferred annuities within the trust. These annuities allow the trust to accumulate income without incurring immediate taxes, and taxes are only owed when the annuity pays out.

Utilizing 1031 Exchanges for Real Estate

For real estate held by the Sigma Trust, a 1031 exchange can allow for tax-deferred growth by deferring capital gains taxes on the sale of a property. Under a 1031 exchange, the trust can sell a property and use the proceeds to purchase a like-kind property without triggering capital gains taxes.

- **Eligibility for 1031 Exchange**: To qualify for a 1031 exchange, the properties involved must be "like-kind," meaning they are of similar nature or character. The trust must follow

strict timelines for completing the exchange
and reinvesting the proceeds.

- **Long-Term Benefits**: By utilizing 1031
  exchanges repeatedly, the trust can defer
  capital gains taxes for an extended period,
  allowing the real estate portfolio to grow
  without immediate tax consequences.

4. Best Practices for Minimizing Tax Liabilities

Implementing best practices in trust management is key
to ensuring that the Sigma Trust remains tax-efficient
over the long term. Below are some strategies to
minimize tax liabilities and maximize the trust's wealth-
building potential:

Implementing Tax-Efficient Investment Strategies

- **Index Funds and ETFs**: The Sigma Trust can
  invest in low-turnover index funds and
  exchange-traded funds (ETFs), which

typically generate fewer taxable events compared to actively managed funds. These investments provide broad market exposure while minimizing capital gains distributions.

- **Tax-Loss Harvesting**: If the trust holds investments that have declined in value, it can sell those investments to offset taxable gains in other areas of the portfolio. This strategy is known as tax-loss harvesting and can help reduce the trust's overall tax burden.

Engaging in Estate Planning

Proper estate planning is critical to minimizing taxes upon the transfer of assets to beneficiaries. The Sigma Trust can utilize estate planning tools such as:

- **Generation-Skipping Trusts**: A generation-skipping trust allows the trust to pass assets to grandchildren or future generations without incurring estate or gift taxes.

- **Grantor Retained Annuity Trusts (GRATs):** GRATs allow the trust's grantor to transfer assets to beneficiaries with minimal gift taxes by retaining an annuity payment for a set period.

Conclusion

Tax efficiency is a cornerstone of trust management for the Sigma Trust. By carefully allocating assets, managing income distributions, and taking advantage of tax-deferred growth opportunities, the trust can significantly reduce its tax liabilities. Through prudent investment strategies, tax-advantaged accounts, and effective estate planning, the trust can protect its assets, build wealth, and ensure long-term sustainability while complying with tax laws. Effective tax management is not only essential for maximizing returns but also for maintaining the trust's financial integrity and achieving its overarching goals.

Section 4: Avoiding Legal Pitfalls and Ensuring Compliance

Ensuring legal compliance is a critical aspect of trust management, particularly for complex structures like the Sigma Trust. While the trust is designed to offer asset protection, tax efficiency, and sovereign-like control, it is essential to navigate the legal landscape carefully to avoid pitfalls and safeguard the trust from invalidation, penalties, or fraudulent activities. This section outlines the key considerations and strategies for avoiding legal pitfalls and maintaining compliance with relevant laws and regulations.

---

1. Trust Documentation and Legal Formalities

The foundation of the Sigma Trust's legality and compliance lies in its documentation. The trust agreement should be meticulously drafted to reflect the true intentions of the grantor while complying with trust law.

Clear Trust Declarations

- **Written Trust Agreement**: A legally binding written trust agreement must be created that outlines the purpose of the trust, the roles and powers of the trustee, and the rights of the beneficiaries. This agreement must be signed and executed by the grantor, trustee, and witnesses as required by law in the trust's jurisdiction.

- **Certification of Trust**: In some cases, a Certification of Trust may be needed. This document serves as a summary of the trust agreement and may be required by financial institutions or legal entities to verify the existence of the trust and its authority to act. This avoids disclosing the entire trust document.

- **State-Specific Requirements**: Different states or countries may have specific requirements for the establishment and management of trusts, including witnessing, notarization, and registration procedures. The Sigma Trust should comply with the applicable jurisdiction's regulations to avoid issues of validity.

Ensuring Legal Language and Definitions

The language of the trust document should be precise and clear to avoid ambiguity or misinterpretation. Common pitfalls include vague or overly broad terms that could undermine the enforceability of the trust or lead to legal disputes. It is crucial to use terminology that complies with legal definitions and is in line with the intended purpose of the trust.

2. Adherence to Tax Laws and Reporting Requirements

Maintaining tax compliance is one of the most crucial aspects of managing the Sigma Trust. Failing to meet tax obligations can result in severe penalties, including the loss of tax-exempt status, fines, or legal action.

- **Trust Tax Identification Number (TIN)**: The Sigma Trust will require a separate TIN (Employer Identification Number, or EIN) to file tax returns and manage financial accounts. The trustee must apply for this number and ensure it is used in all trust-related filings.

- **Income Tax Filings**: Depending on the type of trust, the Sigma Trust may be required to file an annual income tax return, such as Form 1041 in the United States for trusts with income. It's crucial to keep records of all income generated, expenses, and distributions.

- **Reporting Distributions to Beneficiaries**: If the trust distributes income to its beneficiaries, these distributions must be reported on the appropriate tax forms (e.g., Schedule K-1) so that the beneficiaries can accurately report their share of income on their personal tax returns.

- **Compliance with Foreign Asset Reporting**: If the Sigma Trust holds foreign assets or investments, compliance with reporting requirements such as the Foreign Bank Account Report (FBAR) and FATCA (Foreign Account Tax Compliance Act) is essential. Failure to report foreign assets can result in substantial penalties.

Charitable Contributions and Tax Deductions

If the Sigma Trust includes a charitable component, it's important to follow the IRS or applicable country's guidelines for charitable giving. The trust must ensure that any charitable donations are made to qualified organizations, as improper donations can disqualify the trust from benefiting from tax deductions.

- **Qualified Charitable Organizations**: The trust should only make donations to recognized charitable organizations to ensure the deductions are valid.

- **Public vs. Private Charities**: Different tax rules may apply depending on whether the charity is public or private. The trust must be careful to follow the specific guidelines for each type to maximize the charitable contribution benefits.

3. Asset Protection and Fiduciary Duty

One of the main purposes of the Sigma Trust is asset protection. However, improper handling of assets or breaches of fiduciary duty can leave the trust vulnerable to legal challenges and invalidation.

Fiduciary Duties of the Trustee

The trustee of the Sigma Trust has a fiduciary duty to manage the trust's assets in the best interests of the beneficiaries. Failure to uphold fiduciary duties can expose the trustee to personal liability and put the assets of the trust at risk. The trustee's responsibilities include:

- **Duty of Care**: The trustee must manage trust assets with the same degree of care and diligence that a prudent person would use in managing their own affairs.

- **Duty of Loyalty**: The trustee must act in the best interests of the beneficiaries and avoid conflicts of interest. For example, the trustee cannot use trust assets for personal gain or benefit from their position at the expense of the beneficiaries.

- **Duty of Impartiality**: If the trust has multiple beneficiaries, the trustee must act impartially and not favor one over another unless the trust document specifies otherwise.

- **Duty to Avoid Self-Dealing**: The trustee must not engage in transactions that benefit themselves personally. If the trustee benefits from the trust in ways not explicitly outlined in the trust agreement, this could lead to a breach of fiduciary duty.

Avoiding Fraudulent Transfers

One of the most common legal pitfalls for trusts is the fraudulent transfer of assets. If assets are moved into the trust with the intent to defraud creditors or evade legitimate legal obligations, these transfers may be reversed by courts under fraudulent conveyance laws.

- **Reasonable Asset Transfers**: The trust should avoid transferring assets in ways that may appear as attempts to shield assets from legitimate creditors or lawsuits. Transfers must be made in good faith and for valid reasons, such as proper asset protection or estate planning.
- **Documenting All Transactions**: Keeping detailed records of all asset transfers into the trust is essential for proving that they were made for legitimate reasons and not in an attempt to evade creditors.

4. Avoiding Common Legal Pitfalls in Trust Administration

Trusts can face challenges in the administration phase, and common legal pitfalls can lead to disputes, invalidation, or financial loss. Here are some strategies to avoid these issues:

Properly Designating Beneficiaries

Clear beneficiary designations are essential to ensure that the assets of the trust are distributed according to the grantor's wishes. Problems can arise if beneficiary designations are vague, outdated, or not properly updated in the event of life changes (e.g., marriage, divorce, death).

- **Contingent Beneficiaries**: It's important to designate contingent beneficiaries in case the primary beneficiaries predecease the grantor. Without contingent beneficiaries, the assets of the trust may become part of the probate estate.
- **Periodic Reviews**: The trust should be reviewed periodically to ensure that the

beneficiaries listed are still in alignment with the grantor's current wishes.

Regular Trust Administration and Audits

Trust administration should be ongoing and include regular audits to ensure that all trust activities are in compliance with the trust agreement and relevant laws. Failure to perform regular reviews can lead to mismanagement or missed compliance deadlines.

- **Annual Reviews**: An annual review of the trust's financial activities, including income, expenses, distributions, and tax filings, can help ensure everything is operating smoothly.
- **External Audits**: In complex trusts like the Sigma Trust, it may be advisable to hire an independent auditor to review the trust's financial statements to ensure everything is being managed in compliance with legal requirements.

Conclusion

Avoiding legal pitfalls and ensuring compliance is paramount in maintaining the validity, protection, and efficiency of the Sigma Trust. By carefully following the proper documentation, adhering to tax reporting requirements, fulfilling fiduciary duties, and avoiding common legal mistakes, the Sigma Trust can remain a powerful tool for asset protection, tax efficiency, and sovereignty. With careful planning, administration, and legal oversight, the trust will provide lasting benefits to its grantor and beneficiaries while mitigating the risks of legal challenges and invalidation.

Chapter 6: Intellectual Property Management

Section 1: Assigning Copyrights, Trademarks, and Royalties to the Trust

Intellectual property (IP) is a valuable asset that can provide ongoing income streams, recognition, and control. For the Sigma Trust, managing IP assets such as copyrights, trademarks, and royalties is an essential aspect of ensuring financial growth and legal protection. This section outlines the process of assigning intellectual property to the trust, its benefits, and strategies for safeguarding the IP, including the handling of royalties.

1. Overview of Intellectual Property (IP)

Intellectual property encompasses a range of assets that result from creativity, innovation, and branding. The most common types of IP include:

- **Copyrights**: Protection granted to original works of authorship, such as literary works, music, art, and software.
- **Trademarks**: Symbols, words, or other identifiers that distinguish goods or services and represent a brand.
- **Patents**: Legal rights granted to inventors for novel inventions, though these may not always be relevant in a trust focused on copyrights and trademarks.
- **Trade Secrets**: Confidential business information that provides a competitive edge (e.g., formulas, processes, or proprietary data).

By assigning these types of IP to the Sigma Trust, the trust gains ownership of the rights associated with these assets. This offers several benefits, including protection from outside claims, the ability to generate income through royalties, and strategic control over the intellectual property.

2. Assigning Copyrights to the Trust

Copyrights protect the creator's exclusive rights to reproduce, distribute, display, or perform their works. To transfer ownership of copyrights to the Sigma Trust, certain steps must be taken to ensure that the transfer is valid and legally recognized.

Steps to Assign Copyrights to the Trust

- **Create a Formal Assignment Agreement**: The creator (grantor) must draft an assignment agreement that formally transfers ownership of the copyright to the trust. This agreement should include:
    - A description of the work being transferred (e.g., a book, article, song, etc.).
    - A statement that the copyright is being transferred in full (or partially, if applicable) to the Sigma Trust.

- The signatures of the grantor and the trustee, as well as any witnesses or notaries if required.
- **Register the Transfer with the U.S. Copyright Office (if applicable)**: While the transfer of copyright ownership is effective once the assignment agreement is signed, it may be advantageous to record the assignment with the U.S. Copyright Office or the relevant office in your jurisdiction. This provides a public record of the transfer and offers additional legal protections.
- **Include a Licensing Clause**: If the copyright holder (trustee or grantor) wants to retain some control over how the work is used, a licensing agreement can be included in the assignment. This grants the trust exclusive or non-exclusive rights to license the work to third parties, providing the potential for revenue generation while protecting the underlying copyright ownership.

3. Assigning Trademarks to the Trust

Trademarks are valuable assets that symbolize a brand's identity. They can be registered or unregistered, and they serve to protect distinctive symbols, logos, or names associated with goods or services.

Steps to Assign Trademarks to the Trust

- **Draft a Trademark Assignment Agreement**: Similar to copyrights, trademarks can be transferred to the Sigma Trust through a formal assignment agreement. This agreement should clearly state:
  - The trademark being transferred.
  - The scope of the transfer (whether it includes the goodwill of the business associated with the trademark).
  - Any specific limitations or conditions attached to the transfer (if applicable).
- **File the Assignment with the U.S. Patent and Trademark Office (USPTO)**: For U.S. trademark owners, it's essential to record the transfer with the USPTO to update the public record and establish the trust as the new owner of the trademark. This step ensures that the trademark is legally recognized as belonging to the Sigma Trust.
- **Maintain Trademark Use and Protection**: After transferring the trademark, the Sigma Trust must continue to use the trademark in commerce or ensure that it is licensed to others for use.

Failure to use the trademark could result in the loss of rights.
- **Licensing and Royalties**: The Sigma Trust can license the trademark to third parties in exchange for royalties. This generates revenue while maintaining the trademark's legal protection.

---

4. Managing Royalties: Income Streams from IP Assets

One of the primary benefits of assigning copyrights and trademarks to the Sigma Trust is the ability to generate ongoing income streams. Royalties from intellectual property are payments made to the trust in exchange for the right to use copyrighted material or trademarks.

Types of Royalties and Income Streams

- **Copyright Royalties**: These are payments made for the use of a copyrighted work. Common sources of copyright royalties include book sales, music streaming, licensing for film or television use, or reproduction rights for books, art, and software. The trust can manage these royalties, ensuring that income is distributed to beneficiaries, reinvested into the trust, or used for specific purposes as defined in the trust agreement.

- **Trademark Royalties**: When the Sigma Trust owns a trademark, it can license the trademark to third parties in exchange for royalties. For example, a company may pay the trust for the right to use a logo or brand name on products. These royalties provide a steady income stream for the trust while preserving the intellectual property's value and protection.

Tracking Royalties and Payments

- **Royalty Agreements**: The Sigma Trust must enter into licensing or royalty agreements with third parties wishing to use its intellectual property. These agreements should specify:
  - The duration of the royalty arrangement.
  - The percentage or amount of royalties to be paid.
  - Payment terms and conditions.
  - Any restrictions on the use of the intellectual property.
- **Revenue Management**: Royalties should be tracked and documented carefully. The trust will need a system to manage the incoming payments, which can include:

- Using a bank account dedicated to trust royalties.
- Regularly reviewing royalty payments to ensure they are consistent with the terms of the licensing agreements.
- Distributing royalty income to beneficiaries or reinvesting it according to the trust's objectives.

- **Tax Implications of Royalties**: The trust must report any royalty income in accordance with tax laws. If the Sigma Trust generates significant royalties, it must ensure that it meets any relevant tax obligations, including income tax filings and reporting on Schedule K-1 if royalties are distributed to beneficiaries.

5. Benefits of Assigning IP to the Sigma Trust

The transfer of intellectual property to the Sigma Trust provides several key advantages:

- **Asset Protection**: By placing valuable IP assets into the trust, these assets are shielded from personal creditors and third-party claims, as the trust owns the rights to the intellectual property rather than the individual.
- **Tax Efficiency**: Income generated by the intellectual property, such as royalties, can be managed and distributed in a tax-efficient manner, depending on the structure of the trust and applicable tax laws.
- **Control and Legacy**: The Sigma Trust provides a framework for long-term control and management of intellectual property. This ensures that the assets are protected and managed according to the grantor's wishes, even after their passing.

Conclusion

Assigning copyrights, trademarks, and royalties to the Sigma Trust is a powerful strategy for managing intellectual property, generating income, and protecting assets. By formalizing the transfer of IP to the trust, the grantor can safeguard valuable works from potential threats while ensuring that the income from these assets is handled according to their long-term financial and legacy goals. This process requires careful documentation, legal compliance, and regular management to ensure that the intellectual property remains protected and profitable for the trust and its beneficiaries.

Chapter 6: Intellectual Property Management

Section 2: Monetizing Intellectual Property Through the Trust

Monetizing intellectual property (IP) is a key strategy for generating revenue and creating long-term financial stability for the Sigma Trust. By strategically utilizing its intellectual assets, such as copyrights, trademarks, and patents, the trust can unlock multiple income streams. This section explores how the trust can effectively monetize its IP, ensuring compliance, protecting the assets, and maximizing financial benefits.

1. Overview of Monetization Strategies

Monetization refers to the process of generating revenue from intellectual property assets. For the Sigma Trust, monetizing IP can take several forms, including licensing agreements, royalty income, joint ventures, and the direct sale of IP assets. These strategies ensure that the trust's intellectual property is used to its full potential, allowing it to contribute to the trust's financial growth.

Key monetization strategies for intellectual property include:

- **Licensing**: Allowing others to use the intellectual property in exchange for royalties or lump-sum payments.
- **Royalties**: Ongoing payments from third parties for using the IP in specific ways (e.g., media distribution, product branding).
- **Sale of IP**: Selling ownership of intellectual property outright, which may provide an

immediate lump sum but relinquishes future
income from the asset.

- **Joint Ventures**: Collaborating with other
  entities to commercialize the IP, typically
  sharing profits from the venture.
- **Franchising**: Using a trademark or business
  model to allow others to operate under the
  brand, typically involving an upfront fee and
  ongoing royalties.

Each monetization method requires thoughtful
consideration of the trust's long-term goals, the nature of
the IP, and the legal and financial ramifications of the
chosen strategy.

2. Licensing Intellectual Property

Licensing is one of the most common and flexible
methods of monetizing intellectual property. Under a
licensing agreement, the Sigma Trust grants a third party
permission to use its intellectual property in exchange
for compensation, typically in the form of royalties. The
terms of the licensing agreement can vary widely,
depending on the needs of both the trust and the licensee.

Steps to License Intellectual Property

- **Draft a Licensing Agreement**: The trust must create a formal licensing agreement that outlines the terms of the license, including:
    - The specific IP being licensed (e.g., a trademark, copyrighted work, etc.).
    - The territory in which the licensee can operate.
    - The duration of the agreement.
    - The royalty rate or lump sum payment.
    - The scope of the license (exclusive, non-exclusive, or sole license).
    - Any restrictions on how the IP can be used.
- **Negotiation**: Negotiating the licensing terms ensures that the trust receives fair compensation for the use of its IP. Factors such as the IP's market value, the licensee's ability to generate income, and the potential for long-term use should be considered in setting the terms.
- **Monitor Compliance**: After the license is granted, the trust must monitor the licensee's use of the IP to ensure compliance with the terms of the agreement. This may include tracking product

sales, usage, and ensuring that the IP is being used according to the specified terms.
- **Ongoing Royalties**: The most common form of licensing compensation is royalty payments, which are typically a percentage of the revenue generated by the licensee from using the IP. These payments provide the trust with a continuous income stream.

3. Generating Royalties Through IP Usage

Royalties are recurring payments made by third parties for using the trust's intellectual property. These payments can be structured in various ways, such as a fixed fee, a percentage of sales, or a combination of both. Royalties are a vital source of ongoing income for the trust, providing financial support while ensuring that the trust retains control over the intellectual property.

Types of Royalties

- **Flat Fee Royalties**: A fixed fee is paid periodically, regardless of the revenue generated by the use of the IP. This provides predictable income for the trust.
- **Percentage-Based Royalties**: A percentage of the sales generated from the use of the IP is paid

to the trust. This is common in licensing deals for products, music, or media.

- **Advance Royalties**: Some agreements require the licensee to pay an upfront lump sum (advance) against future royalties. This can provide the trust with immediate income and offer financial security.

Collecting Royalties

To effectively collect royalties, the trust must establish clear procedures, including:

- **Royalty Reporting**: The trust should require licensees to provide regular reports on sales or usage of the intellectual property. This ensures transparency and allows the trust to verify that royalty payments are being made correctly.
- **Payment Terms**: The agreement should specify the frequency of royalty payments (e.g., monthly, quarterly, or annually). It's crucial that the trust monitors payments to ensure that they are received on time and in the correct amount.
- **Enforcement**: If a licensee fails to comply with the payment terms, the trust has the right to enforce the agreement through legal means, such as seeking a remedy for breach of contract.

4. Joint Ventures and Collaborations

Another effective way to monetize intellectual property is through joint ventures or collaborations with other companies, individuals, or organizations. In this arrangement, the Sigma Trust partners with another entity to commercialize the IP, typically sharing profits from the venture.

Steps to Form a Joint Venture

- **Define the Role of Each Party**: The trust must define its role in the joint venture, including how the intellectual property will be used and what contribution it will make to the venture. This could involve licensing the IP to the partner or allowing the partner to use the IP in exchange for a share of the profits.
- **Draft a Joint Venture Agreement**: A formal joint venture agreement must be established, which should address:
  - The rights and responsibilities of each party.
  - The distribution of profits and expenses.
  - The duration and terms of the joint venture.

- o Intellectual property ownership and protection clauses.
- **Profit Sharing**: The profits from the joint venture should be divided according to the terms of the agreement. Typically, the trust would receive a percentage of the profits derived from the use of its intellectual property.
- **Licensing the IP Within the Joint Venture**: The trust may also choose to license the IP to the joint venture, ensuring that it receives royalty payments while still sharing in the profits of the broader business operation.

5. Sale of Intellectual Property

In some cases, the trust may decide to sell its intellectual property outright. This is a one-time transaction that provides an immediate lump sum payment but relinquishes future royalties and control of the IP. The sale of IP may be appropriate when the trust seeks a large infusion of capital or no longer needs to retain ownership of the asset.

Steps to Sell Intellectual Property

- **Valuation**: Before selling, the trust should obtain a professional valuation of the intellectual property to ensure that it is sold for a fair price. Factors such as market demand, historical income generated by the IP, and the IP's potential for future use should all be considered in the valuation.

- **Negotiation of Sale Terms**: The trust must negotiate the terms of the sale, including the purchase price, payment structure (e.g., lump sum, installment payments), and any restrictions on the buyer's use of the IP.
- **Finalizing the Sale**: Once the terms are agreed upon, the trust must execute a formal agreement that transfers ownership of the intellectual property to the buyer. This may require filing with the U.S. Copyright Office or the USPTO to record the transfer of ownership.

6. Franchising the Brand

Franchising is another potential monetization strategy for trademarks, particularly for businesses with a strong brand identity. In a franchise agreement, the Sigma Trust allows other individuals or entities to operate a business using the trust's trademark and business model in exchange for an initial franchise fee and ongoing royalty payments.

- **Franchise Disclosure Document (FDD)**: The trust must prepare a Franchise Disclosure Document, which provides potential franchisees with essential information about the business and the franchise opportunity.
- **Franchise Agreement**: A franchise agreement must be drafted, outlining the terms under which the franchisee can use the trust's trademark and business model. This includes the franchise fee, royalty percentage, training, and operational guidelines.
- **Monitoring and Support**: The trust must provide ongoing support to franchisees and monitor their compliance with the franchise agreement to ensure the brand's reputation and financial success.

7. Conclusion

Monetizing intellectual property through the Sigma Trust offers a wealth of opportunities for generating income and protecting assets. Whether through licensing, royalties, joint ventures, or the sale of IP, the trust can strategically leverage its intellectual property to create financial stability. The key to successful monetization lies in drafting clear, enforceable agreements, monitoring

IP usage, and ensuring compliance with the terms of the agreements. By taking a proactive approach to IP management, the Sigma Trust can turn its intellectual property assets into valuable, sustainable revenue streams.

Chapter 6: Intellectual Property Management

Section 3: Legal Protections Against Copyright Infringement

Copyright infringement is a serious concern for creators, especially when the intellectual property is a key asset of the Sigma Trust. Protecting the trust's copyrights and other intellectual property from unauthorized use, reproduction, or distribution is vital for preserving the value of these assets and maintaining financial stability. This section explores the legal protections available to the trust to defend against copyright infringement, as well as the steps it can take to ensure its intellectual property rights are upheld.

1. Understanding Copyright Infringement

Copyright infringement occurs when someone violates the exclusive rights of the copyright holder. These rights include the ability to reproduce, distribute, perform, and create derivative works based on the original work. For the Sigma Trust, these works may include literary creations, artistic works, music, films, or other creative endeavors.

Common forms of copyright infringement include:

- **Unauthorized Reproduction**: Copying the work without permission.
- **Distribution Without Authorization**: Selling or distributing copies of the work without the copyright holder's consent.
- **Derivative Works**: Creating new works based on the copyrighted material without permission.
- **Public Performance or Display**: Using the copyrighted work in public without the proper licensing.

It is essential that the Sigma Trust proactively monitors its intellectual property to detect and address any infringements before they cause substantial financial or reputational damage.

2. Copyright Registration and Enforcement

One of the most important steps the Sigma Trust can take to protect its intellectual property is to register its copyrights. While copyright protection exists automatically upon creation of the work, registration provides significant legal advantages, including the ability to sue for statutory damages and attorney's fees in federal court. Additionally, registering the work serves as an official public record of the copyright ownership, which helps to assert the trust's rights.

Steps to Register a Copyright

1. **Creation of the Work**: The trust must ensure that the work is original and fixed in a tangible form (e.g., written, recorded, or otherwise documented).
2. **Complete the Registration Form**: The Sigma Trust must file a registration application with the U.S. Copyright Office. This application includes basic information about the work, the author, and the date of creation.

3. **Pay the Registration Fee**: The registration process typically requires a fee, which can vary depending on the type of work being registered.
4. **Provide a Copy of the Work**: The trust must submit a copy of the work being registered, either as a physical copy or an electronic version.
5. **Receive the Certificate**: Once the registration is processed, the trust will receive a certificate of registration, which can be used as evidence in court if infringement occurs.

Benefits of Registration

- **Statutory Damages**: Registration allows the trust to pursue statutory damages in court, which can be much higher than actual damages.
- **Attorney's Fees**: If the trust prevails in an infringement lawsuit, it can recover attorney's fees if the work was registered before the infringement occurred.
- **Public Notice**: Registration provides public notice of the copyright, helping to deter potential infringers.

3. Monitoring and Identifying Infringement

Preventing copyright infringement begins with vigilance. The Sigma Trust must actively monitor its intellectual property to detect unauthorized use. There are several tools and strategies available to identify infringement:

- **Search Engines and Online Platforms**: Tools like Google's reverse image search, YouTube's Content ID system, and other monitoring services can help identify when copyrighted content is being used without permission. The trust should periodically search for its works to ensure that they are not being misused.
- **Social Media Monitoring**: Social media platforms are common venues for copyright infringement. The trust can set up alerts or use social media monitoring tools to detect any unauthorized sharing or use of its copyrighted works.
- **Third-Party Monitoring Services**: Several services are designed to help copyright holders monitor the use of their works online. These services can scan websites, digital marketplaces, and platforms to identify infringements on behalf of the trust.

By identifying infringement early, the trust can take swift action to stop the unauthorized use of its intellectual property and minimize financial damage.

---

4. Enforcing Copyrights: Legal Actions Against Infringement

If infringement occurs, the Sigma Trust must take legal action to protect its rights. Copyright enforcement can take several forms, from cease-and-desist letters to formal legal proceedings. It is crucial to follow a structured approach to ensure that the trust's rights are enforced effectively.

Cease-and-Desist Letters

A cease-and-desist letter is often the first step in addressing copyright infringement. The letter notifies the alleged infringer that they are violating the trust's copyright and demands that they immediately stop using the protected work. A well-drafted cease-and-desist letter should include:

- A description of the copyrighted work and the infringing use.

- A request to stop the infringement and remove the work.
- A warning of potential legal action if the infringement is not resolved.

Cease-and-desist letters can often resolve infringement issues without the need for litigation. However, if the infringer refuses to comply, further legal steps may be necessary.

Filing a Lawsuit for Copyright Infringement

If informal efforts do not result in a resolution, the Sigma Trust may need to file a lawsuit for copyright infringement. The trust can pursue legal action in federal court, which has exclusive jurisdiction over copyright disputes.

To file a lawsuit, the trust must prove the following elements:

1. **Ownership of a Valid Copyright**: The trust must provide evidence of the copyright registration or the creation of the work if unregistered.
2. **Infringement**: The trust must prove that the infringer copied or used the work without authorization. This can involve presenting

evidence of the unauthorized use, such as screenshots, documents, or witness testimony.

If successful, the court can grant several remedies, including:

- **Injunctive Relief**: The court can issue an injunction, ordering the infringer to cease using the copyrighted work.
- **Monetary Damages**: The court may award the trust damages for the infringement, which can include actual damages (based on the loss suffered by the trust) or statutory damages (a set amount for each infringement).
- **Attorneys' Fees**: If the trust prevails, the court may award attorneys' fees, reimbursing the trust for legal costs.

Alternative Dispute Resolution (ADR)

In some cases, copyright disputes can be resolved through alternative dispute resolution methods, such as mediation or arbitration. These methods can be less costly and time-consuming than litigation and may be an effective way to reach a settlement without going to court.

---

5. Fair Use and Defenses to Copyright Infringement

It is important for the Sigma Trust to be aware of certain defenses that may be raised by accused infringers. One of the most common defenses is the claim of **fair use**. Fair use allows limited use of copyrighted works without permission for purposes such as criticism, comment, news reporting, education, research, or parody.

The fair use doctrine involves a case-by-case analysis based on several factors, including:

- **Purpose and Character of the Use**: Whether the use is for commercial or non-commercial purposes, and whether it is transformative (adding new expression or meaning).
- **Nature of the Copyrighted Work**: The more factual or noncreative the work, the more likely it may be deemed fair use.

- **Amount and Substantiality**: The extent to
  which the copyrighted work is used,
  including whether the amount used is
  reasonable.
- **Effect on the Market**: Whether the use
  negatively impacts the market for the original
  work or its potential market.

The trust should consult legal counsel to evaluate
whether an accused use qualifies as fair use or whether
further legal action is necessary.

6. Conclusion

Protecting the intellectual property of the Sigma Trust
from copyright infringement is a critical component of
its overall asset protection strategy. By registering
copyrights, actively monitoring usage, and taking swift
legal action when infringement occurs, the trust can
safeguard its creative works and preserve their value.
Legal protections such as cease-and-desist letters,
copyright lawsuits, and awareness of defenses like fair
use are essential tools in maintaining control over the
trust's intellectual property. Ultimately, enforcing

copyrights ensures that the trust's assets remain secure
and continue to generate income for years to come.

Chapter 6: Intellectual Property
Management

Section 4: Growing Intellectual Property
Assets

Intellectual property (IP) is a dynamic and powerful
asset that, when properly managed, can generate
revenue, increase the trust's portfolio, and enhance its
overall financial position. The Sigma Trust must
strategically grow its intellectual property assets to
maximize their value and contribute to long-term
sustainability. This section explores various methods to
grow IP assets, including through creation, acquisition,
licensing, and other strategies, while ensuring that the
trust's IP portfolio remains robust and profitable.

---

1. Creating New Intellectual Property

The most direct way for the Sigma Trust to grow its IP
assets is through the creation of new works. By
continuously producing original content, inventions,

designs, or innovations, the trust expands its intellectual property portfolio. The trust can create a wide range of IP assets, including:

- **Literary Works**: Books, articles, and online content.
- **Artistic Creations**: Paintings, drawings, sculptures, and other visual art.
- **Musical Compositions**: Songs, sound recordings, and musical performances.
- **Software and Technology**: Computer programs, algorithms, and applications.
- **Inventions and Patents**: New devices, processes, or products that are novel and useful.
- **Trademarks and Logos**: Unique names, symbols, and branding elements associated with goods and services.

By creating a diverse range of works, the trust can diversify its IP portfolio and reduce reliance on any single asset. This also allows the trust to benefit from multiple revenue streams, such as royalties, licensing fees, and product sales.

Best Practices for Creation

- **Innovation and Uniqueness**: The trust should prioritize original and innovative works that provide competitive advantages in the marketplace.
- **Documentation**: Ensure that all works are well-documented and legally protected through copyright registration, patent filings, and trademark applications.
- **Continuous Creation**: Developing a pipeline of creative works ensures a constant influx of new intellectual property assets.

---

2. Acquiring Intellectual Property

In addition to creating new intellectual property, the Sigma Trust can expand its IP portfolio by acquiring existing works. Intellectual property acquisition is a powerful strategy to quickly increase the value of the trust's assets. The trust can acquire IP through:

- **Purchasing Copyrights**: Buying the rights to existing literary works, artworks, or other creative content.
- **Acquiring Patents**: Acquiring patents for technologies, inventions, or processes developed by others.
- **Trademark Acquisition**: Purchasing well-established trademarks or logos that have brand value.
- **Licensing Agreements**: Entering into agreements where the trust can purchase the right to use someone else's IP in exchange for a fee or royalty.

Considerations for Acquisition

- **Due Diligence**: Thoroughly research the value and ownership of the IP being acquired to ensure there are no hidden liabilities or disputes.
- **Valuation**: Understand the current market value of the IP and its potential for future

growth. Acquiring valuable IP at a fair price increases the trust's asset base.

- **Revenue Potential**: Prioritize IP that can generate long-term income through licensing, merchandising, or royalties.

By acquiring valuable IP, the trust can instantly increase its portfolio, create additional income streams, and reduce the risks associated with relying solely on its creations.

---

3. Licensing and Monetizing Intellectual Property

Licensing is one of the most effective ways for the Sigma Trust to grow its intellectual property assets while maintaining ownership. Licensing allows the trust to grant others the right to use its IP in exchange for royalty payments, a lump sum, or other financial compensation. This strategy generates passive income and expands the reach of the trust's intellectual property.

- **Exclusive License**: Grants the licensee the exclusive right to use the IP in a particular market or region. The trust may receive upfront payments or royalties in exchange for this exclusivity.
- **Non-Exclusive License**: Allows multiple licensees to use the IP simultaneously, generating additional revenue from multiple sources.
- **Sublicensing**: The trust can grant a licensee the right to sublicense the IP to others, expanding the reach of the IP while generating more revenue.

Best Practices for Licensing

- **Establish Clear Terms**: The trust should clearly define the terms of the license agreement, including the scope, duration, and financial arrangements.

- **Negotiate Royalties**: Ensure that the royalty rates are favorable, and negotiate terms that ensure long-term revenue generation from licensing deals.
- **Monitor Usage**: Regularly track and monitor the use of licensed IP to ensure compliance with the terms and to prevent misuse.

By licensing its intellectual property, the trust can generate revenue without relinquishing ownership or control of the original asset, allowing for the continued growth of its IP portfolio.

4. Leveraging IP for Strategic Partnerships and Collaborations

Another way to grow intellectual property assets is by using existing IP to form strategic partnerships and collaborations. The Sigma Trust can enter into agreements with other businesses, creators, or institutions to expand the value of its intellectual property and benefit from joint ventures.

Types of Partnerships

- **Co-Branding**: Partnering with other brands to jointly market a product or service that incorporates the trust's IP. This can increase visibility and revenue for both parties.
- **Joint Ventures**: Entering into joint ventures with other businesses or organizations to co-develop new products, services, or technologies based on the trust's IP.
- **Franchising**: If the trust owns a strong brand or trademark, it can franchise the business model to other parties who will use the trust's IP to operate their own businesses.

Strategic Benefits

- **Revenue Growth**: Partnerships and collaborations can open up new revenue streams, expand the market for the trust's IP, and generate profits from joint ventures.

- **Market Expansion**: Strategic collaborations allow the trust to reach new audiences, enter new markets, and increase the visibility of its IP.
- **Leverage Expertise**: By collaborating with industry leaders or experts, the trust can enhance the value of its intellectual property and create innovative products or services.

---

5. Protecting and Enhancing IP Value

As the Sigma Trust grows its intellectual property assets, it is essential to continuously protect and enhance the value of those assets. This involves not only defending against infringement but also ensuring that the IP is managed efficiently and its value is maximized.

Ongoing IP Protection

- **Trademark Monitoring**: Regularly monitor the market to detect any unauthorized use of the trust's trademarks. Take legal action if necessary to prevent brand dilution or misuse.

- **Patent Maintenance**: Pay the necessary maintenance fees to keep patents in force and continue to enforce the patent rights against infringers.
- **Copyright Enforcement**: Actively pursue copyright infringement cases and use tools like digital rights management (DRM) to protect digital works.

Enhancing IP Value

- **Branding and Marketing**: Continue to build and promote the trust's brand and trademarks through marketing efforts, which will increase their value in the marketplace.
- **Diversification**: Look for ways to diversify the use of existing IP to create new products, services, or income streams. For example, licensing IP to different industries or expanding into new geographic regions.

6. Conclusion

Growing intellectual property assets is a critical aspect of the Sigma Trust's strategy to increase its wealth and long-term sustainability. By focusing on creation, acquisition, licensing, and strategic partnerships, the trust can significantly expand its IP portfolio and generate continuous revenue streams. Simultaneously, the trust must ensure that its IP is continually protected from infringement and legal challenges, while maximizing the value of these assets through marketing, diversification, and strategic management. With a proactive approach, the Sigma Trust can build a strong foundation of intellectual property that will provide lasting financial and legal benefits.

Chapter 7: Managing Income and Distributions

Section 1: The Trustee's Role in Managing Income Streams

One of the primary functions of the trustee in the Sigma Trust is to effectively manage the income generated by the trust's assets. These income streams may come from a variety of sources, including royalties from intellectual property, investments, business operations, and other financial assets held by the trust. The trustee is responsible for ensuring that these income streams are properly managed to fulfill the trust's objectives while also protecting the interests of the beneficiaries.

---

1. Understanding the Trustee's Fiduciary Duty

The trustee holds a fiduciary duty to act in the best interest of the beneficiaries and the trust's purposes. This responsibility includes making prudent decisions regarding the management, allocation, and distribution of income generated by the trust's assets. The trustee must adhere to legal and ethical standards to ensure the trust is managed in a way that maximizes value and minimizes risk. This includes:

- **Duty of Loyalty**: The trustee must act in the best interest of the trust and its beneficiaries, avoiding any conflicts of interest that could compromise the trust's integrity.
- **Duty of Prudence**: The trustee is obligated to manage the trust's income streams and assets with care, skill, and caution. This includes making informed decisions based on sound financial analysis.
- **Duty of Impartiality**: The trustee must act fairly and impartially toward all beneficiaries, ensuring that no one beneficiary is favored over another in the distribution of income or assets.

These duties form the foundation of the trustee's role in managing income streams.

2. Identifying and Optimizing Income Streams

To effectively manage income streams, the trustee must first identify all the sources of income generated by the trust's assets. This could include:

- **Royalties**: Income generated from intellectual property assets, such as copyrights, patents, trademarks, and licensing agreements.
- **Investment Income**: Earnings from investments in stocks, bonds, real estate, or other financial assets.
- **Business Operations**: Income derived from any businesses owned by the trust or income generated from services provided under the trust's ownership.
- **Rental Income**: Earnings from real property held by the trust, such as rental payments from tenants or lease agreements.

- **Dividends and Interest**: Income from corporate shares, bonds, or other interest-bearing financial assets owned by the trust.

Once identified, the trustee must optimize these income streams by:

- **Maximizing Profitability**: Making decisions that enhance the profitability of the income-generating assets. For example, by renegotiating royalty agreements, maximizing investments, or improving the efficiency of business operations.
- **Diversifying Income Sources**: Ensuring that the trust's income is not overly dependent on any single source. Diversification helps mitigate risk and enhances the trust's financial stability.
- **Monitoring Market Trends**: Staying informed about trends in the marketplace to adjust the trust's income-generating strategies

accordingly, ensuring that the trust benefits from emerging opportunities.

---

3. Allocating and Managing Income for the Trust's Objectives

Income generated by the trust must be allocated according to the trust's specific purposes and the terms outlined in the trust document. For the Sigma Trust, income management and allocation will depend on the goals of asset protection, tax efficiency, and sovereignty. The trustee must:

- **Ensure Alignment with Trust Goals**: All income must be allocated in a manner that furthers the core principles of the Sigma Trust, including asset protection, tax efficiency, and legal sovereignty.
- **Cover Operating Expenses**: Income may need to be allocated for the operational costs of maintaining the trust, including fees for legal services, accounting, asset

management, and other necessary
expenses.

- **Reinvest Income**: The trustee may decide to
  reinvest income back into the trust to
  increase the value of assets or generate
  additional income streams. For example,
  reinvesting in real estate or buying more
  intellectual property assets.
- **Maintain Financial Liquidity**: It is important
  that the trust maintains a sufficient level of
  liquidity to cover immediate expenses,
  opportunities, and any potential legal
  liabilities.

4. Income Distribution to Beneficiaries

As part of the trustee's role, income must be distributed
to the beneficiaries according to the terms outlined in the
trust agreement. The trustee must carefully consider the
needs and interests of each beneficiary before making
any distributions. The distribution strategy will depend
on several factors:

- **Beneficiary Needs**: Some beneficiaries may require a higher income distribution for support, while others may prefer to leave the income reinvested to increase the overall value of the trust.
- **Tax Considerations**: Distributing income to beneficiaries can have tax implications, both for the trust and the beneficiaries. The trustee must carefully consider the tax consequences of each distribution and ensure that the trust remains compliant with tax laws.
- **Frequency and Amount of Distributions**: The trustee may decide on regular distributions (e.g., quarterly or annually) or on an ad hoc basis, depending on the needs of the beneficiaries and the income available.

The distribution process must be carried out in a manner that balances the needs of the beneficiaries with the long-term goals of the trust. Additionally, the trustee must ensure that any income distribution is legally compliant and in line with the trust's purpose.

5. Ensuring Transparency and Record-Keeping

To maintain the integrity of the trust and avoid potential disputes, the trustee must ensure full transparency in managing income and distributions. This involves:

- **Detailed Record-Keeping**: The trustee should maintain accurate and comprehensive records of all income streams, expenses, and distributions. These records should be available for review by beneficiaries and other stakeholders, as required.
- **Regular Reporting**: Providing periodic financial reports to the beneficiaries to keep them informed about the income generated, the allocation of funds, and the status of any distributions.
- **Audit-Proofing**: Keeping all records organized and ready for auditing by legal or

tax authorities, ensuring that the trustee can demonstrate the integrity and transparency of the trust's income management.

6. Conclusion

The trustee plays a critical role in managing the Sigma Trust's income streams and ensuring that income is distributed in a manner that aligns with the trust's core goals of asset protection, tax efficiency, and sovereignty. By identifying and optimizing income sources, allocating funds strategically, and ensuring transparency, the trustee can maximize the trust's financial success while protecting the interests of the beneficiaries. Managing income and distributions with care, foresight, and compliance is essential for the long-term sustainability and growth of the Sigma Trust.

Section 2: Balancing Distributions: Beneficiaries vs. Principal's Needs

In any trust structure, balancing the needs of beneficiaries with the principal's goals and requirements is a critical responsibility for the trustee. For the Sigma Trust, this balance is particularly significant due to the multi-dimensional nature of its capacities, including the legal, spiritual, and personal elements of the trust. The distribution process must respect both the individual needs of the beneficiaries and the overarching purpose of the trust, ensuring its long-term sustainability while supporting the current needs of its beneficiaries.

1. Understanding the Roles of Beneficiaries and the Principal

The Sigma Trust operates with a multifaceted structure where the principal (often referred to as God, or the divine aspect of the trust) represents the ultimate guiding force and the direction of the trust's assets, whereas the beneficiaries represent individuals or entities that will receive benefits from the trust's resources. In balancing distributions, the trustee must consider:

- **Beneficiaries' Needs**: Beneficiaries may be individuals or entities that rely on income or distributions from the trust for support, growth, or other purposes. Their needs could vary widely based on their role in the trust and their financial, personal, or spiritual circumstances.

- **The Principal's Needs**: The principal, as the guiding force of the trust, is often more abstract, involving the long-term purposes and directives of the trust. In this case, the principal's needs are focused on ensuring that the trust serves its core mission and goals, such as asset protection, tax efficiency, sovereignty, and long-term growth.

Both the beneficiaries and the principal hold essential roles, and a careful distribution strategy must be implemented to ensure that both parties' needs are addressed without compromising the trust's overall objectives.

2. Distribution Guidelines: Prioritizing Long-Term Goals

When balancing distributions between beneficiaries and the principal's needs, the trustee should prioritize the long-term viability and purpose of the trust. The following factors should be considered:

- **Trust's Long-Term Vision**: Distributions must align with the trust's mission and purpose. For example, if the trust is designed to preserve wealth for future generations, distributions to beneficiaries should be balanced with the need to reinvest income into the trust's assets, ensuring long-term growth and sustainability.

- **Asset Protection**: The trustee must ensure that distributions do not jeopardize the trust's ability to protect its assets. Premature or disproportionate distributions may reduce the trust's capacity to safeguard assets from creditors, administrative agencies, or other threats.

- **Tax Efficiency**: In balancing distributions, the trustee must be mindful of tax consequences. Distributions made to beneficiaries or used to fund the principal's goals could impact the trust's tax liabilities. The trustee must ensure that the trust remains tax-efficient while fulfilling its obligations to the principal and beneficiaries.

- **Protection Against Fraud and Mismanagement**: The trustee must ensure that distributions are made responsibly, safeguarding the trust from being manipulated or misused. Distributions that favor one group over another or are not aligned with the trust's rules could result in legal or financial consequences, including claims of fraud.

3. Meeting Beneficiaries' Needs

While the principal's needs are fundamental to the trust's purpose, the trustee also must meet the financial and personal needs of the beneficiaries. However, distributions to beneficiaries should be carried out with prudence, based on a clear understanding of each beneficiary's needs, role, and contributions to the trust. Factors to consider include:

- **Beneficiary Financial Support**: If the trust is set up to support beneficiaries financially, the trustee may need to balance periodic distributions to provide for their living expenses, business ventures, or educational needs. These distributions must be aligned with the long-term health of the trust and its objectives.

- **Spiritual or Non-Financial Needs**: For some trusts, such as the Sigma Trust, the beneficiaries may have spiritual, moral, or other non-financial needs. Distributions may take the form of spiritual guidance, educational support, or other benefits that contribute to the beneficiaries' overall well-being, not just financial security.

- **Equitable Distribution**: The trustee must ensure that all beneficiaries are treated equitably. This means distributing income fairly and in accordance with the terms of the trust, avoiding favoritism or discrimination. In some cases, unequal distributions may be justified based on specific provisions in the trust document, but these should be carefully justified and documented.

---

4. Supporting the Principal's Needs:

Ensuring the Trust's Purpose

While fulfilling beneficiaries' needs is critical, the principal's needs and the core goals of the trust must take precedence in the overall strategy for distributions. The trustee must ensure that:

- **Preserving the Trust's Integrity**: The trust's purpose as a means of asset protection, sovereignty, and spiritual alignment must be upheld. Excessive distributions that reduce the trust's capital or move it away from its intended mission could weaken the trust's core integrity.

- **Strategic Use of Income for Principal's Growth**: Distributions that benefit the principal (such as funding the long-term goals of the trust or reinvesting income into its assets) may be necessary to ensure the trust continues to grow and fulfill its purpose over time. This could involve reinvesting income into businesses, intellectual property, or real estate holdings that align with the trust's purpose.

- **Balancing Immediate and Long-Term Needs**: While the principal's needs should be safeguarded, this does not mean that distributions to beneficiaries should be delayed indefinitely. The trustee must find a balance between supporting beneficiaries and ensuring that the trust remains strong and healthy in the future.

5. Structuring Balanced Distributions: A Trustee's Strategy

The trustee must devise a strategy to balance distributions between the beneficiaries and the principal's long-term needs. This strategy may include:

- **Periodic Review**: The trustee should review the needs of the beneficiaries and the current state of the trust regularly. This will help determine if the balance between distributions to beneficiaries and reinvestment into the trust is appropriate or needs adjustment.
- **Flexible Distributions**: Based on the evolving needs of the beneficiaries and the trust's

assets, the trustee can adjust the amount and frequency of distributions. The flexibility allows the trustee to respond to changing financial situations or shifts in the trust's priorities.

- **Beneficiary Agreements**: In some cases, a formal agreement between the trust's beneficiaries and the trustee may be necessary to set clear expectations about how distributions will be handled. This agreement could address the distribution of income, the allocation of funds for special purposes, and the long-term strategic goals of the trust.

6. Conclusion

Balancing the needs of beneficiaries with the principal's goals in the Sigma Trust requires careful and thoughtful consideration. The trustee must weigh the immediate needs of the beneficiaries against the long-term objectives of the trust, ensuring that the trust's integrity is preserved while providing support where necessary. Through strategic, flexible, and prudent distribution practices, the trustee can ensure the trust fulfills its purpose and grows sustainably while supporting its beneficiaries. This careful balance is essential for maintaining the trust's strength, mission, and the well-being of all involved.

Section 3: Protecting the Principal's Lifestyle Through the Trust

The Sigma Trust, as a multifaceted and sovereign structure, is designed to not only protect assets but also ensure the well-being and lifestyle of the principal, often referred to as "God" or the divine element of the trust. One of the key objectives of the trust is to provide a framework for safeguarding the principal's lifestyle by insulating it from external pressures, legal claims, or administrative interference. This section will explore the methods and strategies used to protect the principal's lifestyle through the trust, ensuring both financial security and freedom from external threats.

---

1. The Principal's Sovereign Protection

In the Sigma Trust, the principal holds a unique, sovereign status, often transcending conventional legal frameworks. By establishing the principal as a central, protected entity within the trust, the lifestyle of the principal becomes shielded from many external legal and administrative pressures. The following methods are critical for safeguarding this sovereign position:

- **Sovereign Immunity**: The principal's sovereign status within the trust can potentially invoke principles of sovereign immunity, protecting the principal's assets and lifestyle from unwarranted legal claims or governmental actions. By structuring the principal's relationship to the trust as a unique entity, the principal may be shielded from legal obligations or claims made against them personally, provided the trust is properly executed and respected.

- **Asset Shielding**: Assets held within the trust are protected from being seized by creditors, administrative agencies, or other third parties seeking to enforce claims. By positioning the principal as the central figure, the trust can create a firewall that insulates personal

assets and wealth, preventing external
forces from compromising the principal's
financial security.

- **Privacy Protections**: The trust also protects
  the principal's privacy, as it allows for the
  management of assets and financial affairs
  without direct public exposure. The
  principal's identity and involvement in the
  trust can remain private, further shielding
  them from unnecessary scrutiny or
  exploitation.

2. Ensuring Financial Security for the Principal's Lifestyle

One of the central functions of the Sigma Trust is to
ensure that the principal's lifestyle remains financially
secure, with steady access to income, resources, and
capital for personal use. This is achieved through several
mechanisms:

- **Income Streams and Distributions**: The trust can provide income streams to the principal through strategic investments, intellectual property royalties, business interests, or other assets that generate ongoing revenue. These funds can be used to maintain the principal's standard of living, pay for personal expenses, and support their lifestyle goals.

- **Trust-Funded Expenses**: The trust can pay for personal expenses directly, such as housing, travel, medical care, and education, ensuring that these costs are covered without drawing on personal income or assets that may be vulnerable to external claims. The trustee has the discretion to allocate funds to meet the principal's lifestyle needs, reducing the risk of financial strain.

- **Protection Against Market Volatility**: By strategically managing the trust's investments, the trustee can help the principal maintain a stable financial position even in times of economic downturn or market volatility. This ensures that the principal's lifestyle remains intact regardless of external economic pressures.

3. Legal Protections and the Principal's Lifestyle

In order to protect the principal's lifestyle from potential threats, the Sigma Trust must be carefully crafted to adhere to legal standards that shield both the principal and the trust itself. Several legal mechanisms are involved:

- **Trust Protections Against Creditors**: As a legal entity separate from the principal, the Sigma Trust can be used to protect the principal's assets from creditors, lawsuits, or government actions. Creditors generally cannot seize assets held in trust unless specific conditions are met (such as fraudulent conveyance or personal guarantees), providing the principal with a layer of protection from claims that could disrupt their lifestyle.

- **Avoiding Legal Exposure**: By using the trust structure, the principal's personal assets and financial dealings are kept separate from their personal identity. This separation reduces the likelihood of personal liability in legal disputes, as the trust itself becomes the legal owner of assets, not the principal. Additionally, this structure may reduce the potential for the principal's name and reputation being targeted or damaged in lawsuits or public disputes.
- **Fiduciary Duty of the Trustee**: The trustee has a legal obligation to act in the best interests of the trust and its principal. This fiduciary duty ensures that the principal's lifestyle is protected by directing assets, income, and resources in ways that support

the principal's long-term well-being and financial independence. The trustee must exercise caution in protecting the principal from potential harm or financial distress.

4. Lifestyle Preservation Through Estate Planning

Beyond day-to-day financial security, the Sigma Trust also plays a crucial role in the principal's long-term estate planning, ensuring that the principal's lifestyle and legacy are maintained throughout their lifetime and passed on according to their wishes. Some key aspects of this include:

- **Succession Planning**: The trust can include provisions for the smooth transfer of assets and control to designated beneficiaries or entities upon the principal's passing. This ensures that the principal's lifestyle is preserved and that their assets are passed on in a manner that aligns with their values and goals.

- **Generational Wealth Management**: The Sigma Trust allows the principal to create a long-lasting legacy, with assets growing and being distributed across generations while preserving the lifestyle and values of the principal. The trust structure ensures that wealth is passed down without the risks associated with probate or public legal battles, maintaining privacy and continuity.

- **Charitable Giving and Spiritual Goals**: The principal may use the trust to align their lifestyle with spiritual or charitable objectives, ensuring that their assets are directed towards causes or institutions that reflect their values. This can create a holistic framework where the principal's lifestyle is tied to broader goals beyond personal consumption, including philanthropy and spiritual fulfillment.

5. Strategic Use of the Trust for Lifestyle Flexibility

The Sigma Trust is not only about asset protection; it is also a tool for lifestyle flexibility. Through the use of specific provisions, the principal can ensure they have the freedom to adapt to changing circumstances and opportunities. Key strategies include:

- **Discretionary Distributions:** The trustee can be granted the discretion to make distributions as needed to support the principal's lifestyle, providing flexibility to address new opportunities or needs as they arise. These discretionary powers give the principal the ability to adjust to changing life circumstances without requiring formal modifications to the trust structure.

- **Lifestyle-Linked Investments:** The principal may choose to invest in lifestyle-enhancing assets, such as properties, businesses, or personal interests, through the trust. By doing so, the trust can ensure that the principal's lifestyle is supported while also generating income and growth.

- **Self-Sustaining Lifestyle**: With the right strategies in place, the Sigma Trust can allow the principal to maintain their lifestyle independently of external sources of income. Through asset growth, income from investments, and other resources held within the trust, the principal can achieve a self-sustaining lifestyle that reduces reliance on external income or employment.

6. Conclusion

Protecting the principal's lifestyle through the Sigma Trust involves a comprehensive approach that integrates asset protection, financial security, legal safeguards, and long-term planning. By carefully managing income streams, shielding assets from external threats, and ensuring flexibility, the Sigma Trust enables the principal to maintain their desired lifestyle and financial independence. This structure not only preserves the principal's current way of life but also supports their broader goals and legacy, creating a holistic framework for long-term security and sovereignty.

Section 4: Ethical Considerations in Managing Trust Income

In managing the income generated by the Sigma Trust, it is crucial to uphold ethical standards that align with both legal requirements and the principles of fairness, transparency, and accountability. This section will explore the ethical considerations involved in handling trust income, ensuring that both the principal's interests and the broader community are respected and protected. The management of trust income must reflect a commitment to integrity, responsible stewardship, and the long-term sustainability of the trust.

---

1. Fiduciary Duty and Ethical Stewardship

At the core of the ethical management of trust income is the fiduciary duty of the trustee. The trustee has a legal and ethical responsibility to act in the best interests of the principal and beneficiaries, ensuring that trust income is managed prudently and in accordance with the trust's objectives. Some key ethical responsibilities include:

- **Duty of Care**: The trustee must exercise reasonable care in managing the trust's income and assets. This involves making informed decisions based on due diligence and research, ensuring that the income generated is sustainable and aligned with the trust's long-term goals.
- **Duty of Loyalty**: The trustee must act solely in the interests of the trust and its beneficiaries, avoiding any conflicts of interest. Any personal gain or outside influence that could compromise the trustee's judgment must be avoided. Ethical stewardship requires putting the trust's best interests first, without self-dealing or prioritizing external interests.
- **Duty of Prudence**: The trustee must manage the trust's income in a way that preserves and grows the trust's assets. This includes

making investments and decisions that
balance risk and reward, ensuring that the
principal's lifestyle is supported while also
safeguarding the long-term financial health
of the trust.

2. Transparency and Accountability in Income Management

Transparency and accountability are fundamental ethical
principles in managing trust income. The trustee must
provide clear and regular reporting to all relevant parties,
ensuring that the management of the trust's income is
visible, traceable, and aligned with the established goals.
This includes:

- **Regular Financial Reporting**: The trustee
  should provide regular, detailed reports on
  the income generated by the trust, as well as
  how those funds are allocated. This helps
  ensure that the principal, beneficiaries, and
  other stakeholders are informed about the

financial status of the trust and the performance of its assets.

- **Clear Documentation of Decisions**: Every decision regarding income management should be documented, including the reasoning behind investment choices, distribution decisions, and any actions taken to protect or grow the trust's income. This documentation ensures that the trustee's actions are ethically justifiable and can be reviewed if necessary.

- **Auditing and Oversight**: To further promote accountability, the trust can engage independent auditors or establish an oversight mechanism that reviews the trust's financial activities. This serves as an additional safeguard against mismanagement and ensures that the trustee is held to ethical standards.

3. Balancing Income with the Trust's Social and Ethical Goals

While the principal's lifestyle and financial needs are central to the Sigma Trust, the ethical management of trust income also involves considering the broader impact of income generation and allocation. The trust can incorporate social, environmental, and ethical considerations into its investment strategy and income distribution, ensuring that the trust not only benefits the principal but also aligns with a broader ethical vision. Some ethical considerations include:

- **Social Responsibility**: The trust may choose to allocate income towards socially responsible investments, such as supporting businesses or initiatives that promote sustainability, human rights, or ethical practices. This approach ensures that the trust's wealth generation aligns with values beyond pure financial gain.
- **Charitable Contributions**: The trust can incorporate provisions for charitable giving, directing a portion of the income towards

causes that align with the principal's values
and spiritual goals. This ensures that the
trust contributes to the well-being of others,
fulfilling a broader ethical purpose beyond
individual financial benefit.

- **Environmental Sustainability**: As part of
  ethical income management, the trust can
  prioritize investments in environmentally
  sustainable industries or projects. This
  ensures that the trust's income generation
  supports long-term ecological health and
  minimizes harm to the planet, reflecting an
  ethical commitment to sustainability.

4. Ethical Income Distribution and Fairness

In addition to how income is generated, ethical
considerations must also be made regarding how income
is distributed among the principal, beneficiaries, and
other parties involved in the trust. The distribution of
income must be fair, transparent, and consistent with the

goals of the trust, ensuring that all stakeholders are treated equitably. Key aspects include:

- **Fair and Just Distribution**: The trustee must ensure that income distributions are made fairly, respecting the intentions of the trust and the needs of the beneficiaries. The trustee should avoid favoritism or unequal treatment, ensuring that each beneficiary's share is consistent with the trust's objectives and legal framework.

- **Principle of Need**: If the trust provides income to beneficiaries beyond the principal, ethical considerations should ensure that income is distributed according to the needs of the beneficiaries. This may include factoring in financial hardship, health needs, or other personal circumstances, ensuring that the income distribution process is compassionate and fair.

- **Avoidance of Exploitation**: Ethical income management involves ensuring that no party, including the principal, is financially exploited through excessive distributions or improper use of the trust's income. The trustee must maintain a balance between meeting the principal's lifestyle needs and preserving the long-term sustainability of the trust for future generations.

5. Avoiding Conflicts of Interest and Self-Dealing

One of the most critical ethical considerations in managing trust income is the prevention of conflicts of interest and self-dealing. The trustee must be vigilant in avoiding situations where personal interests could compromise their fiduciary duties. Some practices to maintain ethical integrity include:

- **Prohibition of Self-Dealing**: The trustee must avoid using the trust's income for personal gain or benefiting from transactions that would financially benefit them at the expense of the trust or its beneficiaries. Ethical management of trust income requires full transparency and a commitment to acting in the best interests of the principal and the trust.

- **Independent Advice and Consultation**: When making decisions regarding income management, the trustee should seek independent financial and legal advice to ensure that their decisions are unbiased and made with the trust's best interests in mind. This helps mitigate the risk of conflicts of interest and ensures that the trustee's actions are ethically sound.

- **Disclosure of Interests**: If the trustee has any personal or financial interest in the trust's income-generating activities, they must disclose this to the principal and beneficiaries. Full disclosure ensures that all stakeholders are aware of any potential

conflicts and can make informed decisions
regarding the trust's management.

Conclusion

The ethical management of trust income is central to the
integrity and success of the Sigma Trust. By adhering to
fiduciary duties, maintaining transparency, aligning
income strategies with ethical values, and ensuring
fairness in income distribution, the trustee can ensure
that the trust serves both the principal's needs and
broader ethical objectives. The careful and ethical
management of income not only preserves the trust's
financial health but also aligns the trust's actions with its
values, ensuring that it remains a responsible and
sustainable entity in the long term.

Section 1: Legal Protections Embedded in the Sigma Trust

In today's increasingly complex legal and administrative environments, safeguarding against administrative fraud is a critical consideration when designing a trust. The Sigma Trust is built to offer robust legal protections, ensuring that its assets, intellectual property, and income streams remain secure from governmental and institutional overreach or fraudulent actions. This section will outline the key legal protections embedded within the Sigma Trust and explain how these protections contribute to a fortified defense against administrative fraud.

---

1. Shielding the Trust from Governmental Overreach

One of the primary concerns for individuals seeking to protect their assets through a trust is the risk of government interference or overreach. The Sigma Trust includes several legal mechanisms to reduce the risk of government or administrative agencies claiming control over the trust's assets:

- **Irrevocability of the Trust**: One of the strongest protections against government seizure is the irrevocable nature of the Sigma Trust. Since the assets within the trust are no longer legally considered the property of the trust's creator (the principal), they cannot be easily accessed or confiscated by governmental agencies. This ensures that once assets are transferred into the trust, they are protected from administrative claims and creditors.
- **Cestui Que Vie Trust Structure**: Incorporating a Cestui Que Vie trust structure further shields the trust from administrative intrusion. Under this arrangement, the trust is positioned as an independent legal entity, protecting it from government actions designed to seize assets or impose liabilities. The principle of "life" under the Cestui Que Vie structure emphasizes the notion that the principal's rights and assets are protected as long as the trust remains in effect.
- **Divesting Personal Ownership**: The trust allows for the legal divestment of personal ownership over assets, effectively transferring the control and management of the assets to the trust. This separation of personal and trust ownership limits the ability of administrative agencies to claim or manipulate the assets under the guise of personal liability or taxation.

2. Trustee as a Safeguard Against Mismanagement and Fraud

The trustee of the Sigma Trust plays an integral role in safeguarding against administrative fraud and ensuring that the trust's assets are protected from both external and internal threats. The trustee's duties and responsibilities serve as an additional layer of protection:

- **Fiduciary Duty of the Trustee**: The trustee is legally bound by fiduciary duties to act in the best interests of the trust and its beneficiaries. This includes managing the trust's assets with care, loyalty, and impartiality. The trustee must ensure that all transactions are legitimate and transparent, protecting the trust's integrity and preventing any fraudulent activity.
- **Third-Party Oversight**: Independent oversight and auditing are integral to the Sigma Trust's fraud prevention strategy. The trustee can engage external parties to periodically review the trust's activities, ensuring that all actions are compliant with legal standards and that there are no signs of fraud or mismanagement.
- **Asset Segregation**: Assets held by the trust are segregated from other personal or business accounts, ensuring that they are protected from being co-mingled or accessed by unauthorized

parties, including government agencies. This segregation is crucial in maintaining the distinction between personal and trust-owned assets, offering further protection from administrative fraud.

3. Legal Clauses and Provisions to Prevent Fraudulent Claims

The Sigma Trust includes specific legal clauses designed to prevent fraudulent claims and protect the trust's assets from administrative overreach. These provisions ensure that the trust's management remains free from unlawful interference:

- **Anti-Fraud Clauses**: These clauses explicitly outline the procedures to be followed in the event of a fraudulent claim against the trust. They empower the trustee to challenge any such claims in court, ensuring that the trust is not subject to administrative fraud or exploitation.
- **Notice Requirements**: Any claim or interference by an administrative agency must be formally notified and substantiated with clear evidence. The trust's clauses ensure that all claims made against the trust are subject to strict scrutiny before they can proceed, allowing for legal

defenses to be raised in the event of fraud or wrongful claims.

- **Injunction Clauses**: If there is a threat of fraudulent claims or unlawful actions by an administrative agency, the trust contains clauses that allow for immediate injunctive relief. This provides a legal mechanism to stop any potential fraudulent action or seizure of assets before it can take place.
- **Jurisdiction Clauses**: The Sigma Trust includes jurisdiction clauses that stipulate the appropriate legal venue in which disputes will be resolved. This ensures that any claims or legal actions against the trust will be handled in a jurisdiction that is favorable to the trust's protection, thereby reducing the risk of fraudulent claims arising from administrative agencies in other jurisdictions.

4. Documentation and Record-Keeping for Fraud Prevention

Transparent documentation and meticulous record-keeping are essential components of the Sigma Trust's strategy for protecting its assets from administrative fraud. The trust ensures that all transactions, including transfers of assets, distributions, and income streams, are

well-documented and easily accessible for auditing or
legal review:

- **Comprehensive Record-Keeping**: The trust
  mandates the maintenance of detailed records for
  all financial activities, including income
  generation, distributions, and any legal actions
  taken in relation to the trust. These records are
  kept up to date and are securely stored to prevent
  tampering or misrepresentation.
- **Public Records of Ownership**: As part of the
  transparency of the Sigma Trust, records related
  to intellectual property, trademarks, copyrights,
  and other assets held by the trust are made
  available through public registries or filing
  systems. This provides a transparent trail of
  ownership and reduces the likelihood of
  fraudulent claims regarding ownership.
- **Auditing and Compliance Tracking**: The trust
  ensures that regular audits are conducted by
  independent parties, focusing specifically on the
  protection of the trust's assets and the prevention
  of fraud. Audits also serve as a defense in case
  administrative agencies attempt to challenge the
  trust's legitimacy.

5. How These Protections Mitigate the Risk of Fraud

By embedding robust legal protections into the Sigma Trust, the principal can mitigate the risk of fraud and undue interference by administrative agencies. These protections serve multiple functions, from shielding assets to ensuring transparency and compliance with the law. Some of the key benefits include:

- **Minimizing Exposure to Government Seizure**: By establishing the trust as a separate legal entity, the assets held within the trust are less vulnerable to government or agency actions that might otherwise seize personal property or income streams.
- **Preserving Privacy**: Legal provisions and the use of separate entities, such as the Cestui Que Vie structure, help maintain the privacy of the trust's assets and financial activities. This reduces the likelihood of administrative agencies or creditors identifying vulnerabilities to exploit.
- **Strengthening Legal Defenses**: The combination of anti-fraud clauses, fiduciary duties, and independent oversight provides a robust defense against any fraudulent claims or administrative actions. In the event of a challenge, the trust is positioned to present a strong, legally defensible position.

Conclusion

The Sigma Trust is designed with multiple layers of legal protections that not only ensure the preservation of assets and income streams but also provide powerful safeguards against fraudulent actions by administrative agencies. Through the use of irrevocability, anti-fraud clauses, independent oversight, and comprehensive record-keeping, the trust is equipped to defend against a variety of legal challenges. These protections offer peace of mind to the principal, knowing that their assets are secure from unlawful interference, and ensure that the trust operates in alignment with its founding principles.

Section 2: Administrative Fraud Tactics and How to Counteract Them

Administrative fraud, a form of illicit manipulation or exploitation by governmental or institutional entities, poses a significant threat to those seeking to safeguard their assets and financial resources. This section will explore common administrative fraud tactics that individuals and entities often encounter, particularly in the context of asset protection trusts, and will outline effective strategies to counteract these tactics using the legal framework of the Sigma Trust.

1. Common Administrative Fraud Tactics

Administrative agencies, by virtue of their authority and resources, often engage in practices that can undermine individual rights, exploit loopholes in the law, or unlawfully access assets. The following are common tactics used by administrative agencies in attempts to compromise trust-based protections:

a. Unwarranted Seizure of Assets

Government entities may initiate proceedings to seize assets under the guise of tax collection, debt recovery, or regulatory compliance, often without clear justification. They may claim that assets within a trust belong to the individual in question, ignoring the legal separation between the principal and the trust itself.

b. Illegitimate Claims of Ownership or Control

Administrative fraud can take the form of claiming ownership or control over intellectual property, real estate, or other assets held within a trust, typically using ambiguous or manipulated legal documents or statutes. This tactic may involve claiming that the trust does not have legal standing or that the assets in question are under the control of the government due to alleged tax delinquencies or other perceived violations.

c. Regulatory Overreach and Bureaucratic Manipulation

Administrative agencies can engage in overreach by enforcing unnecessary or overly broad regulations that directly affect a trust's operations. For example, agencies may demand excessive documentation, impose punitive taxes, or apply regulatory measures that restrict the trust's ability to function in accordance with its foundational purpose.

d. Fraudulent Tax Liens and Garnishments

In some cases, administrative agencies may place fraudulent tax liens or garnishments on a trust's income or assets. These actions are often based on erroneous or manipulated information designed to exploit the trust for financial gain. This is a common tactic used in cases where agencies seek to recover funds without properly examining the legal status of the trust.

e. False Reporting and Misrepresentation of Facts

Administrative agencies may engage in fraudulent activities by falsifying reports or misrepresenting facts regarding the trust's financial activities, ownership, or tax obligations. This could involve creating fabricated documents or providing misleading information to the court or financial institutions.

---

2. Counteracting Administrative Fraud:

Legal Defenses and Protective Measures

The Sigma Trust provides a robust framework for addressing and counteracting these common tactics. Below are effective countermeasures that can be employed to protect against administrative fraud:

a. Irrevocability Clause to Prevent Seizure

The irrevocable nature of the Sigma Trust offers one of the strongest defenses against unwarranted seizure of assets. When assets are transferred into the trust, they are no longer legally considered the property of the individual principal. By ensuring that the trust is irrevocable and assets are formally designated as trust property, the principal can prevent administrative agencies from attempting to seize or control these assets under fraudulent claims.

- **Countermeasure:** If an administrative agency attempts to seize assets, the trust's irrevocability clause and Cestui Que Vie structure can be invoked to show that the assets are legally protected and belong to the trust, not the individual. This protects the assets from unjust governmental interference.

b. Clearly Defined Ownership and Control Structures

Administrative fraud often involves confusion or misrepresentation of asset ownership. To prevent this, the Sigma Trust includes precise legal documentation specifying the trust's ownership of intellectual property, real estate, and other assets.

- **Countermeasure**: All assets within the Sigma Trust, including trademarks, copyrights, and real estate, should be clearly documented and filed with the relevant legal entities or registries. This ensures there is an official public record of the trust's ownership, making it difficult for administrative agencies to claim ownership or control.

c. Jurisdiction Clauses and Venue Selection

To protect against regulatory overreach, the Sigma Trust includes clauses specifying the jurisdiction and venue where any disputes or claims related to the trust will be resolved. This serves as a proactive defense against administrative agencies operating outside of the agreed-upon legal parameters.

- **Countermeasure**: If an administrative agency attempts to apply unnecessary or irrelevant regulations to the trust, jurisdiction clauses can be invoked to ensure that the dispute is handled in a favorable legal environment. Additionally, these clauses reduce the risk of the trust being subject to arbitrary regulatory enforcement.

d. Anti-Fraud and Audit Provisions

The Sigma Trust incorporates robust anti-fraud provisions that enable the trustee to challenge any fraudulent claims or actions taken by administrative agencies. These clauses empower the trustee to resist fraudulent tax liens, garnishments, or claims of ownership, ensuring that the trust's assets remain protected.

- **Countermeasure**: The trustee can use these provisions to initiate legal actions against fraudulent tax liens, garnishments, or other claims imposed by government agencies. By demonstrating the legitimacy of the trust and its assets, the trustee can prevent the unlawful seizure of funds or property.

e. Comprehensive Record-Keeping and Transparency

One of the best ways to counteract fraudulent claims is to maintain clear, organized records that demonstrate the legitimacy of the trust's assets and activities. The Sigma Trust mandates comprehensive record-keeping to ensure that every transaction, asset transfer, and financial activity is well-documented and transparent.

- **Countermeasure**: In the event of a fraudulent claim, the trustee can present detailed records to challenge the claims made by administrative agencies. This documentation provides an irrefutable legal defense, demonstrating that all activities within the trust are legitimate and in compliance with relevant laws.

f. Legal Precedents and Case Law

The Sigma Trust is structured with a clear understanding of existing legal precedents related to asset protection and trust management. By staying informed of relevant case law, the trust can proactively address potential legal challenges from administrative agencies.

- **Countermeasure**: Should an administrative agency attempt to initiate fraudulent claims, the trust's legal counsel can draw upon established case law to dispute the validity of the agency's actions. This ensures that the Sigma Trust is built on sound legal principles that protect it from unlawful interference.

3. Using the Sigma Trust to Protect Against Fraud

Incorporating these strategies and protections into the Sigma Trust framework provides a robust defense against administrative fraud. The combination of legal safeguards, such as irrevocability, anti-fraud clauses, and clear ownership structures, helps ensure that the trust remains secure from both external fraud and governmental overreach.

The trust's ability to separate personal assets from trust assets, its use of the Cestui Que Vie structure, and its emphasis on transparency and compliance make it an invaluable tool for protecting one's wealth, intellectual property, and resources from fraudulent administrative practices.

4: Conclusion

Administrative fraud can undermine the security of personal and business assets, but with careful planning and the right legal protections in place, individuals can protect their interests from governmental overreach and manipulation. The Sigma Trust's robust legal framework, including irrevocability, anti-fraud provisions, and asset segregation, offers a powerful defense against administrative fraud, ensuring that trust assets are secure and that the principal's rights are protected. By implementing these strategies, individuals can effectively safeguard their wealth, intellectual property, and income streams, while maintaining full legal compliance with applicable laws and regulations.

Section 3: Using the Trust Protector for Oversight and Defense

The role of the **Trust Protector** is an increasingly vital component of modern trust structures, especially when the goal is to ensure long-term asset protection and defense against external threats, including administrative agencies, creditors, and other potentially harmful actions. In the context of the Sigma Trust, the Trust Protector acts as an oversight and defense mechanism to provide an additional layer of security for the trust's assets, ensuring that the intentions of the principal are respected and that the trust remains protected from manipulation or legal challenges.

This section will explore the role of the Trust Protector, how to incorporate this figure into the Sigma Trust framework, and how it can be strategically used to guard against administrative fraud and ensure the trust's longevity and integrity.

1. The Role of the Trust Protector

A **Trust Protector** is an independent third-party entity or individual appointed to oversee the administration of the trust, making certain that the terms of the trust are being upheld and that the principal's objectives are being achieved. Unlike the trustee, who is directly responsible for managing the trust's assets and day-to-day operations, the Trust Protector's role is more advisory and supervisory in nature. The Trust Protector has the ability to intervene when necessary to safeguard the trust's interests.

Key Responsibilities of the Trust Protector:

- **Ensuring Compliance:** The Trust Protector ensures that the trustee is adhering to the terms of the trust and complying with the law. They can step in if they believe the trustee is acting in a way that might jeopardize the trust's assets or the principal's goals.

- **Protecting Against Fraud and Overreach:** The Trust Protector can act as a safeguard against fraudulent claims, especially those coming from administrative agencies or external parties attempting to access the trust's assets.

- **Modification and Amendment Power:** In some cases, the Trust Protector has the power to modify or amend the terms of the trust in order to adapt to unforeseen circumstances, such as changes in law, taxation, or new threats to the trust's stability.
- **Dispute Resolution:** In cases of conflict between the trustee and beneficiaries or other parties, the Trust Protector may serve as a neutral third party to mediate and resolve disputes, ensuring that the trust continues to operate smoothly.

2. Trust Protector Powers in the Sigma Trust

The **Sigma Trust** can include various powers for the Trust Protector to enhance its defensive capabilities, especially in relation to administrative fraud. These powers are designed to provide a dynamic, flexible defense structure, allowing the Trust Protector to intervene proactively in situations where fraud, regulatory overreach, or other challenges threaten the integrity of the trust.

a. Right to Remove and Replace the Trustee:

The Trust Protector has the power to remove and replace the trustee if they believe the trustee is failing to act in the best interest of the trust or is being influenced by external pressures (such as government agencies or creditors). This power provides an important safeguard against mismanagement and administrative interference.

- **Example**: If a government agency attempts to place a lien or garnish trust assets without proper cause, the Trust Protector could remove the current trustee and replace them with someone who is better equipped to defend against these actions.

b. Discretionary Powers to Modify the Trust:

The Trust Protector may have the discretion to modify certain terms of the trust to better align with evolving laws or unexpected threats. For example, if an administrative agency introduces a new regulation that threatens the trust's operations, the Trust Protector could amend the trust to better protect it from such overreach.

- **Example**: The Trust Protector could modify the trust's provisions regarding asset distribution or reporting requirements to protect against tax-related penalties or regulatory encroachment.

c. Veto Power Over Trustee Decisions:

The Trust Protector may have veto power over certain trustee decisions, particularly those involving significant financial transactions or changes to the structure of the trust. This can prevent the trustee from making decisions that could put the trust's assets at risk.

- **Example**: If the trustee is considering transferring significant assets out of the trust in a way that could leave the principal vulnerable to claims by administrative agencies, the Trust Protector could veto this decision, preventing such a move.

d. Appointment of Successor Trust Protectors:

To ensure the trust's continued protection, the Trust Protector can have the power to appoint a successor. This ensures that the trust remains under proper oversight even in the event that the original Trust Protector is unable to perform their duties.

- **Example**: In the case of incapacitation or resignation of the Trust Protector, a successor could be appointed immediately to continue oversight without any gap in protection.

3. Strategic Use of the Trust Protector in Defending Against Administrative Fraud

In the context of the **Sigma Trust**, the Trust Protector becomes a key figure in ensuring that the trust's assets remain protected from fraudulent claims or administrative overreach. The Trust Protector's oversight role ensures that if any threats to the trust's integrity arise, there is a responsive mechanism in place to defend against them.

a. Protecting Against Unlawful Seizures and Garnishments:

If an administrative agency attempts to seize or garnish assets held in the trust under fraudulent claims, the Trust Protector can intervene by reviewing the legitimacy of the agency's actions and stopping them if necessary. By ensuring the trust's compliance with the law, the Trust Protector can protect against unlawful asset seizure.

- **Example**: If the IRS or another governmental agency attempts to garnish royalties or other assets held by the trust, the Trust Protector can challenge the legality of such actions and, if appropriate, direct the trustee to take legal action to contest the garnishment.

b. Defending Against Regulatory Overreach:

Regulatory bodies often attempt to impose rules or restrictions that go beyond their legal authority. The Trust Protector can act as a check on these regulatory bodies, ensuring that the trust is not subject to unnecessary or illegal interference. This protection is particularly important for trusts that hold intellectual property, as these assets are often targeted by governmental entities.

- **Example**: If a state or federal agency attempts to impose an unconstitutional regulation on intellectual property held by the trust, the Trust Protector could review the situation and, if needed, take legal action to challenge the regulation or modify the trust's structure to protect the intellectual property from regulatory interference.

c. Mitigating the Risk of Fraudulent Tax Liens:

Administrative fraud can often involve fraudulent tax liens, especially when the trust's income or assets are being mischaracterized or improperly taxed. The Trust Protector can prevent such liens by ensuring that the trust is complying with all legal requirements and that any fraudulent claims by tax authorities are contested in court.

- **Example**: If a tax authority places an incorrect or fraudulent lien on trust assets, the Trust Protector can ensure that the lien is contested and removed, preventing the trust from being penalized for erroneous claims.

4. Conclusion: Empowering the Sigma Trust with the Trust Protector

The Trust Protector is an essential figure within the **Sigma Trust**, offering crucial oversight and defensive capabilities that enhance the trust's protection against external threats, particularly administrative fraud. By ensuring compliance, overseeing trustee decisions, and acting as an independent authority, the Trust Protector can safeguard the trust's assets and ensure the principal's intentions are fully realized. Incorporating the Trust Protector into the trust framework provides a dynamic layer of security that strengthens the trust's ability to withstand challenges and protect the wealth and resources held within it.

Through strategic use of the Trust Protector's powers, the **Sigma Trust** can more effectively shield itself from fraudulent claims, regulatory overreach, and other risks that might compromise the integrity of the trust. This ensures that the principal's assets remain safe, secure, and in line with their long-term objectives, providing peace of mind and stability for generations to come.

Section 4: Building an Anti-Fraud Infrastructure

Creating a robust anti-fraud infrastructure is a critical component of ensuring the Sigma Trust remains secure from fraudulent claims, administrative overreach, and external threats. Fraud, whether through misrepresentation, unauthorized claims, or unlawful interference, can undermine the integrity of the trust and compromise the assets it holds. Building a comprehensive anti-fraud infrastructure within the Sigma Trust ensures that not only are the trust's assets protected but that the trust operates with full transparency, compliance, and accountability.

This section will focus on the steps necessary to establish an anti-fraud infrastructure that shields the trust from fraudulent activities and administrative exploitation, using a combination of legal safeguards, best practices in governance, and proactive measures to defend the trust's assets.

1. Legal Framework for Fraud Prevention

The first layer of protection against fraud within the Sigma Trust is the establishment of a strong **legal framework**. This framework includes provisions in the trust document that explicitly outline measures to prevent and respond to fraud, as well as an understanding of how the trust will engage with potential fraudulent activities.

Key Components of a Legal Anti-Fraud Framework:

- **Clear Provisions for Fraudulent Claims**: The trust document should specify procedures for identifying and responding to fraudulent claims, particularly those that might originate from administrative agencies, creditors, or other external parties. These provisions can set a clear pathway for the trustee to contest such claims in court or through other legal means.

- Example: If an administrative agency fraudulently claims ownership of trust assets or attempts to impose undue taxes or penalties, the trust document may include language specifying that any such claim must be substantiated through a legal proceeding before the agency can take action.
- **Indemnification Clauses**: Including indemnification clauses in the trust can protect trustees and other fiduciaries from personal liability arising from actions taken in good faith to protect the trust from fraud. This ensures that trustees are not discouraged from taking necessary actions to defend the trust's assets.
- **Fraudulent Transfer Protection**: In some jurisdictions, creditors may attempt to seize assets that were fraudulently transferred into a trust. To mitigate this risk, the Sigma Trust should include provisions that demonstrate legitimate transfers of assets into the trust, with documentation proving that such transfers were made for lawful purposes.
- **Dispute Resolution Clauses**: A comprehensive dispute resolution process should be built into the trust, including arbitration, mediation, or even judicial intervention. These mechanisms allow the trust to handle claims of fraud or challenges

to the trust without leaving room for ambiguity or
protracted litigation.

2. Governance Best Practices

Beyond the legal structure, establishing **best practices in
governance** is essential to preventing fraudulent
activities. Strong governance ensures that the actions of
the trustee, beneficiaries, and other stakeholders are
transparent, well-documented, and compliant with all
applicable laws.

Best Practices for Governance to Prevent Fraud:

- **Regular Audits and Reviews**: Conducting
  regular audits of the trust's activities and assets is
  a key safeguard against fraud. An independent
  auditor or an internal auditing system can help
  ensure that no unauthorized transactions or
  actions are taken. Audits should be scheduled
  annually and should include reviews of all
  financial transactions, asset movements, and
  compliance with trust provisions.
- **Transparency and Documentation**: All trust
  transactions should be fully documented and
  easily accessible for review. This transparency
  helps prevent fraudulent actions by creating a

clear paper trail that can be traced and verified if
necessary.

- o **Example:** If the trust holds significant
  intellectual property assets, detailed
  records of licenses, royalties, and
  ownership should be maintained to
  prevent anyone from falsely claiming
  those assets or misappropriating
  them.
- **Independent Oversight**: Appointing
  independent advisors or a Trust Protector can
  provide oversight to ensure that the trustee is
  performing their duties ethically and in the best
  interest of the trust. Regular reviews by these
  independent parties provide an additional layer of
  protection against fraud.

---

3. Proactive Monitoring Systems

In addition to legal provisions and governance structures,
implementing **proactive monitoring systems** can
significantly reduce the risk of fraud. Monitoring
systems track the trust's assets, financial transactions,
and any potential external threats, such as administrative
interference or fraudulent claims.

Effective Monitoring Systems for Anti-Fraud

Protection:

- **Asset Tracking**: Use technology to track and monitor the assets held by the trust. For example, intellectual property assets like copyrights and trademarks can be monitored through automated systems that alert the trust of any unauthorized use, infringement, or challenges to ownership.
- **Financial Transaction Monitoring**: Regularly monitor all financial transactions, especially those involving large sums of money or assets. Automated systems can alert the trustee to any unusual activity that might indicate fraudulent activity or mismanagement.
- **Legal and Regulatory Watch**: Stay up to date with legal and regulatory changes that could affect the trust. Monitoring any new laws or government regulations that impact asset protection, intellectual property, or administrative powers can help the trust proactively adjust its strategies.

4. Crisis Response and Fraudulent Claim Management

Even with a robust anti-fraud infrastructure, there may be instances where a fraudulent claim is made against the trust. In such cases, it is essential to have a clear **crisis response** plan that outlines how to handle such situations effectively and efficiently.

Steps in Crisis Response and Fraudulent Claim Management:

- **Immediate Legal Action**: If a fraudulent claim is made, the trustee should be prepared to act swiftly. This includes consulting with legal counsel to prepare a defense and, if necessary, initiating legal proceedings to contest the fraudulent claim. The Trust Protector may also be brought in to oversee the defense and provide guidance on how to proceed.
- **Documentation of Fraudulent Claims**: All communications and documents related to fraudulent claims should be thoroughly documented. This evidence will be critical in defending the trust's position and countering false claims.
- **Public Communication**: If the fraudulent claim has the potential to impact public perception of the trust, a carefully crafted public statement may

be necessary. This statement should clarify the trust's position and outline the steps being taken to protect its assets.

- **Collaboration with Law Enforcement**: In cases of severe fraud or administrative overreach, it may be necessary to involve law enforcement. The trust should be prepared to cooperate with authorities to ensure that any fraudulent activity is investigated and prosecuted to the fullest extent of the law.

---

5. Conclusion: A Strong, Fraud-Resistant Trust

Building a strong **anti-fraud infrastructure** is essential to ensuring that the Sigma Trust remains a secure and reliable structure for asset protection, income management, and legal sovereignty. By incorporating a comprehensive legal framework, governance best practices, proactive monitoring systems, and a clear crisis response strategy, the trust can effectively defend against fraudulent activities and administrative fraud.

With these protections in place, the Sigma Trust can operate with confidence, knowing that it is fortified against external threats and able to protect its assets for the benefit of the principal, beneficiaries, and future generations.

Section 1: Key Clauses to Strengthen the Sigma Trust

To ensure the Sigma Trust operates effectively and is protected from both internal and external threats, it is essential to include strategic **clauses** in the trust document. These clauses serve as the foundational protections that safeguard the trust's assets, define the roles and responsibilities of those involved, and clarify the operational framework of the trust itself. They also establish the rules for the administration of the trust, creating a legal safeguard against unauthorized actions, fraudulent claims, or potential exploitation. By including the right clauses, the trust can ensure that it remains legally robust, transparent, and secure.

In this section, we will explore the **key clauses** that should be incorporated into the Sigma Trust to strengthen its legal and protective framework. These clauses ensure that the trust remains intact, respects the wishes of the principal, and effectively defends against external risks, including administrative interference, creditor claims, and fraudulent activities.

1. Irrevocability Clause

One of the most essential clauses in an irrevocable trust is the **irrevocability clause**. This clause affirms the trust's permanent nature, indicating that once assets are transferred into the trust, they cannot be removed or revoked without following the established legal procedures. The irrevocability clause provides a strong protection against administrative interference and ensures the trust's stability over time.

Key Features of an Irrevocability Clause:

- **Affirmation of Permanence**: Explicitly states that the trust is irrevocable and cannot be altered or terminated by the settlor, ensuring that no external party (including government agencies or creditors) can demand the return of assets.
- **Transfer of Assets**: Once assets are transferred, they belong to the trust, and the settlor no longer has direct control over them.
- **Protection from Reversal**: The clause guarantees that the assets placed into the trust are protected from being seized or reallocated by external parties, providing long-term asset protection.

2. Spendthrift Clause

The **spendthrift clause** is crucial for protecting the assets of the trust from being seized by creditors or beneficiaries who may have personal financial issues. It ensures that the assets within the trust cannot be used to satisfy any personal debts or obligations of the beneficiaries.

Key Features of a Spendthrift Clause:

- **Creditor Protection**: Prevents creditors from accessing trust assets, even if the beneficiaries face financial difficulties or legal judgments against them.
- **Discretionary Distributions**: The trustee has the discretion to make distributions, ensuring that the beneficiaries cannot claim a right to the trust assets and thus making the trust's assets inaccessible for creditor claims.
- **Encourages Responsible Use of Trust Assets**: The trustee's discretion helps to ensure that trust funds are used for the

intended purposes and are not misused by beneficiaries.

---

3. Anti-Fraud Clause

An **anti-fraud clause** is essential in protecting the trust from fraudulent activities or any attempts to illegally seize trust assets. This clause provides a clear framework for addressing fraudulent actions, both from internal and external sources, and establishes legal remedies for any fraudulent claims or actions taken against the trust.

Key Features of an Anti-Fraud Clause:

- **Fraudulent Transfers**: Specifies that any transfers of assets made with the intent to defraud creditors or other parties will be void and subject to legal action.
- **Legal Recourse**: Provides the trust with the right to pursue legal action in the event of fraud, including the possibility of recovering

assets that were fraudulently transferred or
misappropriated.

- **Transparency and Accountability**: Ensures
that all actions taken by the trustee and the
beneficiaries are fully documented and
transparent, reducing the risk of fraudulent
activity within the trust.

4. Protection Against Administrative
Interference Clause

A **protection against administrative interference
clause** ensures that the trust's assets and operations are
shielded from interference by governmental or
administrative agencies. This is particularly important
for trusts involved in asset protection and those that may
be targeted by government regulations or claims.

Key Features of the Protection Against
Administrative Interference Clause:

- **Safeguards Trust Assets**: Prevents government agencies or administrative bodies from seizing or interfering with the trust's assets without a lawful court order.
- **Prevents Unlawful Claims**: Ensures that the trust is not subjected to arbitrary claims by governmental or administrative agencies seeking to challenge or seize trust assets.
- **Sovereignty Clause**: Establishes the trust's autonomy and sovereignty, making clear that the trust's operation and its assets are outside the jurisdiction of any unauthorized administrative action.

---

5. Trustee's Powers and Duties Clause

The **trustee's powers and duties clause** defines the scope of the trustee's authority, ensuring that the trustee has sufficient powers to manage, protect, and distribute the trust's assets, while also being held accountable for their actions. This clause ensures that the trustee's actions align with the trust's goals and that they are legally responsible for managing the trust in the best interests of the beneficiaries.

Key Features of the Trustee's Powers and Duties Clause:

- **Authority to Act**: Clearly outlines the trustee's power to make decisions regarding the management, protection, and distribution of trust assets, including the ability to handle investments, monitor intellectual property, and distribute income.
- **Duty of Care and Loyalty**: Ensures that the trustee must act in the best interests of the trust and beneficiaries, avoiding conflicts of interest and self-dealing.
- **Accountability and Oversight**: Requires the trustee to provide regular reports and updates on the trust's activities and

performance, allowing for transparency and oversight by beneficiaries or a Trust Protector.

---

6. Successor Trustee Clause

A **successor trustee clause** ensures that the trust remains operational in the event that the original trustee can no longer serve. This clause designates a successor trustee to take over the trust's management, ensuring continuity and stability in the trust's administration.

Key Features of a Successor Trustee Clause:

- **Designation of Successors**: Specifies who will take over the role of trustee if the original trustee becomes incapacitated, deceased, or otherwise unable to fulfill their duties.
- **Powers and Duties of Successors**: Clearly defines the powers and responsibilities of the successor trustee, ensuring that they are

equipped to manage the trust effectively and
protect its assets.

- **Trust Protector Role**: A Trust Protector may
  be designated to oversee the succession
  process, ensuring that the transition is
  smooth and in line with the trust's goals.

7. Discretionary Distribution Clause

A **discretionary distribution clause** grants the trustee
discretion over how and when assets are distributed to
the beneficiaries, providing flexibility to ensure that the
trust is managed in the most effective way possible. This
clause is important for ensuring that trust assets are used
responsibly and in accordance with the principal's
wishes.

Key Features of a Discretionary Distribution Clause:

- **Flexibility in Distribution**: The trustee has the
  discretion to decide the amount, timing, and
  method of distributions, ensuring that the
  trust's funds are allocated based on the

needs and circumstances of the
beneficiaries.

- **Protecting the Principal**: By giving the trustee
  discretion, the clause helps protect the
  principal's assets from misuse or improper
  claims by beneficiaries.
- **Needs-Based Distributions**: Distributions
  may be made based on the needs of the
  beneficiaries, ensuring that the assets are
  used for their intended purposes, such as
  education, healthcare, or other important life
  needs.

---

8. Amendment Clause (if applicable)

While irrevocable, the trust document may still contain
provisions for **amendments** in certain circumstances.
This allows for adjustments to the trust without
compromising its foundational principles, such as
protecting against fraud or addressing unforeseen legal
changes.

Key Features of an Amendment Clause:

- **Limited Amendments**: Specifies that amendments can only be made under specific circumstances and typically require the approval of a Trust Protector or other designated authority.
- **Alignment with Legal Changes**: Allows the trust to adapt to changes in the law, without undermining its irrevocability or asset protection features.

Conclusion

The inclusion of these key clauses will fortify the Sigma Trust, ensuring that it operates smoothly, securely, and in alignment with the principal's wishes. These clauses not only strengthen the trust legally but also provide the flexibility and protections necessary to navigate challenges, avoid administrative interference, protect assets, and ensure long-term financial security for beneficiaries. As you draft and finalize the Sigma Trust, carefully incorporating these clauses will help safeguard its integrity, longevity, and success in fulfilling its intended purposes.

Section 2: Authenticity Mechanisms:

Preventing Fraudulent Misuse of the Trust

The integrity of the Sigma Trust depends not only on the robustness of its legal framework but also on the authenticity mechanisms it employs to prevent fraudulent misuse. The trust, as a valuable and sophisticated legal instrument, must be protected from potential manipulation, fraud, or unauthorized actions that could undermine its goals. Whether it involves external threats from fraudulent actors or internal threats from individuals with access to the trust, maintaining the authenticity of the trust is paramount for its success.

This section will explore the **authenticity mechanisms** within the Sigma Trust that are designed to safeguard it against misuse and ensure that its operations remain aligned with its original intent. These mechanisms focus on authentication protocols, oversight structures, and legal strategies that prevent the trust's resources from being diverted, abused, or exploited by unauthorized parties.

1. Trust Authentication Protocols

To prevent fraudulent misuse of the trust, it is critical to establish stringent **authentication protocols** for any action related to the trust, such as the transfer of assets, distribution of income, and changes to the trust's structure. These protocols ensure that only legitimate actions, authorized by the trust's legal documents, are carried out.

Key Features of Trust Authentication Protocols:

- **Signature and Document Verification**: All documents related to the trust (including transfers, amendments, and distributions) should be verified with secure signatures or digital authentication tools to ensure their legitimacy. This includes using **notaries**, **witnesses**, and **secure digital signatures** that can be independently verified.

- **Identification and Validation**: To prevent unauthorized parties from accessing trust resources, protocols must include methods for **identifying trustees**, **beneficiaries**, and

other authorized persons through personal identification or other verifiable data.

- **Audit Trails**: Maintaining **audit trails** is critical for ensuring that all trust-related actions are traceable and verifiable. Every transaction or decision made regarding the trust should be recorded, with detailed logs that can be reviewed by a Trust Protector, auditor, or legal professional to ensure that everything is legitimate and in line with the trust's objectives.

2. Role of the Trust Protector in Preventing Fraud

The **Trust Protector** is an essential figure in safeguarding the authenticity of the Sigma Trust. This individual is responsible for ensuring that the trust is administered according to its terms and that any fraudulent activity or misuse of the trust is detected and addressed swiftly. The Trust Protector serves as a neutral party with the authority to intervene if the trustee or any other party attempts to misuse or defraud the trust.

Key Features of the Trust Protector's Role:

- **Oversight of Trustee Actions**: The Trust Protector has the power to oversee the actions of the trustee, ensuring that all actions taken are in accordance with the trust's intent and legal framework. If the Trust Protector detects any misconduct or breach of fiduciary duty, they can intervene or remove the trustee.

- **Dispute Resolution**: The Trust Protector can serve as a mediator or arbitrator if there are disputes regarding the trust's administration. This role ensures that conflicts are resolved in a way that preserves the authenticity of the trust and prevents potential misuse.

- **Veto Power**: In cases of significant changes to the trust or its operations (e.g., asset transfers, amendments), the Trust Protector may have the veto power to prevent actions that could compromise the trust's purpose or authenticity. This gives the Trust Protector the authority to prevent fraudulent or unauthorized activities before they can take place.

---

3. Safeguarding Against False Claims and Identity Theft

One of the most critical threats to the authenticity of the Sigma Trust is **fraudulent claims** and **identity theft**. In particular, the misuse of the trust's name, assets, or associated intellectual property could result in substantial harm. Preventing such misuse requires implementing strategies to ensure that no one can claim false ownership or attempt to exploit the trust's resources without legitimate authority.

Key Features of Safeguarding Against Fraudulent Claims:

- **Trademark and Copyright Protection**: The trust should proactively register its **intellectual property**—including trademarks, copyrights, and patents—to prevent unauthorized use or fraudulent claims. This registration acts as a public declaration of ownership and can provide legal recourse if the trust's intellectual property is misused.

- **Identity Protection**: Given the potential for fraud related to the principal's name and identity, robust measures should be taken to protect personal information. This can include registering the principal's name as a trademark or setting up digital identification protocols to protect against impersonation.

- **Legal Action Against Fraudulent Claims**: If any fraudulent claim is made against the trust or its assets, the trust should include provisions for immediate legal action. This can involve pursuing claims for damages, stopping fraudulent transactions, and taking steps to ensure that any unauthorized claims are nullified.

---

4. Digital and Physical Security Measures

In the modern world, both **digital** and **physical** security are necessary to protect the authenticity of the trust. Fraud can occur through hacking or unauthorized physical access to documents or assets. A combination of **cybersecurity** measures and **physical security protocols** can prevent external actors from exploiting vulnerabilities.

Key Features of Digital and Physical Security Measures:

- **Cybersecurity Measures**: The trust's digital records, including bank accounts, intellectual property, and other key assets, should be protected by strong **encryption**, **multi-factor** authentication, and **regular security audits**. This ensures that no unauthorized parties can access or manipulate digital information related to the trust.

- **Physical Security**: Important trust documents should be securely stored in **fireproof safes** or **secure vaults** to prevent unauthorized physical access. Regular monitoring and limited access to these physical records further safeguard the trust's authenticity.
- **Digital Asset Management**: If the trust holds digital assets (e.g., cryptocurrency, intellectual property), the digital keys and access rights should be stored in highly secure wallets, with multi-layered security features to prevent theft or unauthorized access.

5. Authentication Through Trust Documentation

All **trust documentation** must be authentic, precise, and verifiable to prevent fraudulent use. This includes having clearly defined **terms of the trust**, **witnesses**, and **signatories** to validate its legitimacy. Additionally, any amendments or modifications to the trust should be accompanied by clear documentation and verification steps.

Key Features of Trust Documentation:

- **Clear Language and Specificity**: The trust should use clear, unambiguous language to define its terms, ensuring that there are no grey areas that could be exploited by fraudulent parties.
- **Witnessed and Notarized Signatures**: All trust-related documents should be signed in front of legally authorized witnesses and notarized to establish their validity.
- **Public Record and Filing**: For added protection, certain trust documents can be

filed with appropriate **public authorities** or **government registries**, where they can be verified by interested parties to confirm authenticity.

6. Periodic Audits and Third-Party Oversight

Another mechanism for maintaining the trust's authenticity is conducting **periodic audits**. These audits, typically performed by a **trusted third-party** accountant or auditor, ensure that the trust's activities are properly documented and that there are no discrepancies or unauthorized actions taking place. Third-party oversight provides an independent check on the integrity of the trust's administration and can detect potential fraud before it becomes a larger issue.

Key Features of Audits and Third-Party Oversight:

- **Independent Auditors**: Engaging professional auditors to periodically examine the trust's operations, financials, and documentation ensures that everything is being handled

according to legal requirements and best
practices.

- **Transparency and Accountability**: Audits
  provide transparency to both beneficiaries
  and third parties, showing that the trust is
  being administered ethically and legally. Any
  discrepancies or fraudulent activities can be
  flagged and addressed immediately.
- **Internal Checks and Balances**: The trust
  should also have **internal review systems** in
  place, where multiple individuals or entities
  are involved in decision-making processes,
  reducing the likelihood of fraudulent actions.

Conclusion

The authenticity mechanisms embedded within the
Sigma Trust are critical for preventing fraudulent
misuse, protecting assets, and maintaining the trust's
integrity. By implementing strong **authentication
protocols**, leveraging the **Trust Protector's oversight**,
safeguarding against **false claims and identity theft**,

and ensuring **digital and physical security**, the Sigma Trust can remain a powerful tool for asset protection and long-term financial stability. These mechanisms not only deter potential fraud but also provide legal recourse should any threats arise, ensuring that the trust operates in alignment with its principal's goals and is safeguarded from any fraudulent activity.

Section 3: Advanced Protection Strategies for Assets and Intellectual Property

The Sigma Trust, as a sophisticated legal structure, provides a solid foundation for asset and intellectual property protection. However, to truly safeguard these assets from both internal and external threats—whether administrative, legal, or financial—advanced protection strategies must be employed. These strategies go beyond basic asset safeguarding and involve innovative and proactive measures that strengthen the trust's defenses and optimize its potential for wealth preservation and growth.

This section will delve into advanced strategies that can be implemented within the Sigma Trust to protect both tangible and intangible assets, with a particular focus on intellectual property. The strategies include cutting-edge legal mechanisms, financial tools, and proactive asset management techniques that ensure robust protection.

1. Establishing a Layered Defense for Intellectual Property

Intellectual property (IP) is a vital asset for many individuals and organizations, often representing a significant portion of wealth. Protecting IP within the Sigma Trust requires a multi-layered defense strategy to prevent theft, unauthorized use, or infringement. This defense framework combines legal tools, strategic asset placement, and ongoing monitoring to create a comprehensive shield around IP.

Key Components of Layered IP Protection:

- **Trademark and Copyright Registrations**: The first line of defense for any intellectual property is ensuring that it is properly registered with the relevant authorities. This includes **trademarks** for brand names, logos, and slogans, as well as **copyrights** for creative works such as written content, artwork, and digital media. Registration provides legal proof of ownership and allows the trust to take action against infringers.
- **IP Holding Companies**: To provide further protection, the trust may establish an **IP holding company**. This company, which is a subsidiary or separate entity owned by the trust, is designated solely for holding the intellectual property assets. This separation provides an

additional layer of legal protection by isolating IP from other assets in the trust and making it more difficult for creditors, attackers, or administrative agencies to claim ownership or control over it.

- **Non-Disclosure and Non-Compete Agreements**: For intellectual property that involves sensitive business ideas, designs, or processes, the trust should require all relevant parties—such as employees, contractors, or collaborators—to sign **non-disclosure agreements (NDAs)** and **non-compete clauses**. These contracts legally bind the parties to maintain confidentiality and prevent them from using proprietary information for personal gain or competing interests.

- **Constant Monitoring and Enforcement**: Intellectual property protection does not end with registration. The trust should invest in regular **monitoring** of the market and online platforms to identify potential infringements. This may include tracking unauthorized use of trademarks or copyrighted content on websites, social media, or marketplaces. Automated tools and third-party services can help flag potential violations, enabling timely enforcement actions.

2. Using Trust-Based Entities for Asset Protection

One of the most effective ways to protect assets—both tangible and intangible—is through the strategic use of **trust-based entities**. These entities can shield the trust's assets from legal claims, creditors, or administrative agencies. By using multiple entities under the Sigma Trust's umbrella, assets are spread across different structures that work together to enhance protection and ensure privacy.

Key Entity Structures for Asset Protection:

- **Family Limited Partnerships (FLPs)**: An FLP is a partnership structure in which the trust holds general and limited partnership interests. It provides a means for transferring ownership of assets while maintaining control over them. FLPs can protect assets from creditors by making it difficult for them to claim ownership of limited partnership shares.
- **Offshore Trusts and Companies**: For individuals looking to expand their protection globally, **offshore trusts** and **companies** can be established in jurisdictions that offer strong asset protection laws, such as the **Cook Islands** or **Nevis**. These structures provide additional layers of confidentiality, legal protection, and financial

freedom. Offshore structures may also help reduce the risk of administrative interference from local government agencies.

- **Real Estate Holding Trusts**: If the trust holds real estate, using a **real estate holding trust** can provide liability protection. This type of trust is designed to hold real estate assets and shield them from legal claims or judgments. It can also help maintain privacy by separating the property ownership from the trust's principal.
- **Spousal Trusts and Irrevocable Trusts**: For married individuals, **spousal trusts** can help protect assets by designating one spouse as the trustee and another as the beneficiary. This setup may provide tax benefits while keeping assets separate from potential claims against either spouse. Additionally, **irrevocable trusts** remove assets from the grantor's ownership, making them less vulnerable to creditors and legal claims.

3. Strategic Use of Insurance for Asset Protection

Insurance plays a vital role in providing a layer of financial protection for both physical and intangible assets. While insurance alone cannot replace a comprehensive asset protection plan, it can serve as a crucial safety net in the event of unforeseen legal or financial issues. The Sigma Trust can benefit from tailored insurance policies that protect its assets and intellectual property from a wide range of risks.

Key Insurance Strategies for Asset Protection:

- **Intellectual Property Insurance**: This type of insurance provides coverage against legal costs related to IP infringement, including defense costs and damages. The trust should consider policies that cover legal defense and compensation for intellectual property disputes, particularly if the IP is a significant asset within the trust.
- **Liability Insurance**: **General liability insurance, errors and omissions insurance**, and **directors and officers insurance** (for trust officers and trustees) provide coverage against claims of negligence, breach of duty, or liability arising from trust management. These policies can be structured to cover both physical and intellectual property-related risks.
- **Umbrella Insurance**: This broader coverage provides an extra layer of protection above and beyond existing insurance policies. Umbrella insurance can help cover large liabilities and claims that may exceed the limits of existing policies, particularly useful for high-value assets and IP.

- **Cybersecurity Insurance**: For digital assets such as proprietary software, websites, and online brands, **cybersecurity insurance** can protect the trust from risks associated with data breaches, hacking, and cyberattacks. The Sigma Trust should consider such policies to protect against digital theft, intellectual property theft, and loss of reputation.

4. Trust Agreements with Protective Clauses

To further enhance asset protection, the Sigma Trust should include **protective clauses** within its trust agreements. These clauses help prevent fraudulent claims, avoid unnecessary legal disputes, and ensure that the trust's assets are protected in the long term.

Key Protective Clauses to Include in Trust Agreements:

- **Spendthrift Clauses**: This clause prevents beneficiaries from using trust assets to satisfy personal debts or liabilities, thus protecting the assets from creditors. A **spendthrift provision** can ensure that the assets of the trust are preserved for future generations or for the intended purposes of the trust.

- **No-Contest Clauses**: To deter beneficiaries from contesting the terms of the trust, a **no-contest clause** can be included. This clause stipulates that if a beneficiary challenges the trust's terms in court and loses, they forfeit their right to any distributions.

- **Discretionary Distribution Clauses**: These clauses give the trustee discretion in deciding how and when to distribute trust assets. This can help prevent assets from being distributed to individuals who may be at risk of financial mismanagement or creditor claims. The trust may also have the power to delay distributions if a beneficiary is facing legal action.

- **Asset-Partition Clauses**: These clauses allow the trust to partition its assets into different segments, each with its own protections, thus reducing the likelihood that a single creditor could claim the entire trust's assets. For example, intellectual property might be held in a separate entity from real estate or financial assets, ensuring that one asset class does not jeopardize the others.

5. Long-Term Planning and Continuity

To ensure that the protection strategies remain effective in the future, the Sigma Trust should incorporate **long-term planning** and **continuity provisions** into its structure. This ensures that the trust remains viable and protected even as circumstances change.

Key Features of Long-Term Planning:

- **Succession Planning**: The trust should include provisions for succession planning, identifying the next trustee or executor to take over if the current trustee becomes unavailable or incapable of performing their duties. This ensures continuity and prevents administrative issues.
- **Periodic Reviews and Updates**: Protection strategies should be regularly reviewed and updated to account for changes in laws, technology, and personal circumstances. The trust should mandate periodic evaluations of its asset protection mechanisms, ensuring that they remain robust and effective.
- **Estate and Legacy Planning**: The trust should align its asset protection strategies with long-term estate planning goals, ensuring that future generations or beneficiaries continue to benefit from protected assets. This includes strategies for passing on intellectual property, investments, and other wealth-preserving measures.

Conclusion

Advanced protection strategies for assets and intellectual property within the Sigma Trust go beyond the basic level of legal protection. By employing a **multi-layered defense** approach, using **strategic entities**, **insurance**, **protective clauses**, and **long-term planning**, the Sigma Trust can ensure that its assets are well-secured against potential threats. These strategies not only safeguard the trust's financial health but also provide a comprehensive framework that minimizes risk and maximizes the protection of both tangible and intangible assets over time.

Section 4: Customizing the Sigma Trust for Maximum Flexibility

The Sigma Trust is designed to be a powerful and adaptable legal structure, offering not only protection for assets but also flexibility in how those assets are managed, distributed, and used over time. One of the key advantages of the Sigma Trust lies in its ability to be customized to suit the unique needs and objectives of its principal and beneficiaries. By tailoring various elements of the trust, the principal can ensure that the trust remains agile in response to changing circumstances while maintaining its core protective and operational functions.

This section will explore how to customize the Sigma Trust for maximum flexibility, providing strategic options for adjusting the trust's terms, management, and beneficiary distributions, all while maintaining its integrity and purpose.

1. Tailoring the Trust's Terms for Specific Objectives

One of the primary customization options for the Sigma Trust is the ability to design its terms in a way that aligns with the specific goals of the principal. By customizing the trust's structure, the principal can adjust how assets are managed, protected, and distributed to beneficiaries, ensuring the trust meets both immediate needs and long-term aspirations.

Key Customization Options:

- **Purpose-Specific Trusts**: The trust can be customized to serve specific purposes, such as education, healthcare, business investments, or legacy preservation. By setting clear objectives, the trust's terms can reflect the purpose behind the assets, ensuring that they are used in the most effective way possible.

- **Flexible Distributions**: The trust can allow for discretionary distributions, which give the trustee the flexibility to make decisions about when and how assets are distributed to beneficiaries. This can include provisions that allow the trustee to consider the beneficiary's financial needs, current circumstances, or even personal growth goals. For example, distributions can be tailored to support education, healthcare, business ventures, or retirement.

- **Adjusting the Beneficiary Structure**: The Sigma Trust can be customized to include a variety of beneficiaries, with specific provisions that allow for future changes. The principal can include provisions that allow new beneficiaries to be added over time, such as future generations or charitable organizations. Additionally, the trust can be designed with specific rules regarding the distribution to beneficiaries, prioritizing those in greater need, ensuring that certain conditions are met, or fulfilling particular objectives, such as charitable causes or family wealth preservation.

---

2. Strategic Amendments and Modifications

Although the Sigma Trust is an irrevocable trust, it can still be structured to provide flexibility through strategic amendments and modifications. These adjustments can be made when circumstances change, ensuring that the trust remains relevant and functional as the principal's situation evolves.

Options for Amendments and Modifications:

- **Trust Protector Clause**: The inclusion of a **trust protector** within the trust agreement provides the ability to make specific amendments to the trust's terms without altering its irrevocable nature. The trust protector acts as an intermediary, with the authority to modify certain provisions of the trust to adapt to unforeseen circumstances or evolving legal conditions. This could include modifying the distribution schedule, adding new beneficiaries, or addressing changes in tax laws or regulations.
- **Decanting the Trust**: Another flexibility tool is the ability to "decant" the trust. This process involves transferring assets from an existing trust to a newly established one, with revised terms. Decanting can be used to address changes in tax laws, evolve the trust's purpose, or improve asset protection. This is an advanced tool often used when the original trust terms need updating without creating the need for judicial intervention or litigation.
- **Distribution Flexibility for Beneficiaries**: The trust can also provide flexibility in how distributions are made. For example, it can

include provisions that allow the trustee to make either **discretionary** or **mandatory** distributions depending on the circumstances. For discretionary distributions, the trustee has the power to decide when and how much to distribute, taking into account the beneficiary's needs, while mandatory distributions require the trustee to distribute a specific amount to the beneficiary at a certain time.

---

3. Incorporating Alternative Asset Structures

One of the unique aspects of the Sigma Trust is its ability to incorporate a wide variety of asset structures, ensuring that the trust is not confined to traditional investment strategies or asset types. By allowing for creative structures, the principal can leverage alternative assets to create diverse income streams, enhance asset protection, and ensure long-term growth.

Alternative Asset Structures:

- **Private Investment Entities**: The Sigma Trust can be customized to hold assets in the form of private investment entities, such as limited liability companies (LLCs) or partnerships. These entities allow the trust to manage assets such as real estate, private equity investments, or other business ventures. By pooling assets in these entities, the trust can reduce its exposure to individual creditor claims and benefit from additional liability protection.

- **Cryptocurrency and Digital Assets**: The rise of digital assets such as **cryptocurrencies** and **NFTs (Non-Fungible Tokens)** provides an opportunity for the Sigma Trust to adapt to the digital age. These types of assets can be incorporated into the trust, ensuring that the principal's digital wealth is protected and managed effectively. The trust can include provisions for the custody and management of these digital assets, including the creation of secure wallets and appointing a trusted digital asset custodian.
- **Intellectual Property as an Asset Class**: The trust can be customized to manage and protect various forms of intellectual property (IP), such as patents, copyrights, trademarks, and trade secrets. These IP assets can be assigned to the trust, where they can be monetized, licensed, or sold to generate revenue streams. The trust can ensure that these valuable assets are carefully managed, protected from infringement, and effectively used to benefit the principal and beneficiaries.
- **Real Estate and Land Holdings**: Real estate can be another key asset class within the Sigma Trust, especially when using specialized real estate holding entities. The trust can include provisions for purchasing, managing, and leasing

real estate properties, thereby ensuring that the assets are protected and generating income.

---

4. Privacy and Confidentiality Provisions

A critical component of customizing the Sigma Trust for maximum flexibility is the ability to ensure privacy and confidentiality. Privacy is essential for asset protection, as it helps shield both the trust's assets and its beneficiaries from unnecessary scrutiny by third parties, including creditors, administrative agencies, and the general public.

Privacy Customization Options:

- **Anonymous Ownership Structures**: The trust can be customized to include **anonymous ownership** structures for assets, particularly real estate and intellectual property. This can be accomplished by using nominee entities, which own the assets on behalf of the trust, allowing the true owner (the principal) to remain confidential.
- **Non-Disclosure Provisions**: Non-disclosure clauses can be incorporated into the trust to ensure that sensitive information about the trust's assets, management, or beneficiaries is not made public. These clauses can be extended to any third parties involved with the trust, such as

financial advisors, accountants, or lawyers, to
prevent information leakage.
- **Confidential Trustee**: The trust can include a
confidential trustee, who may not be a public
figure or easily identifiable, ensuring that the
trust's operations and its management of assets
remain private. This trustee would act in the best
interest of the principal and beneficiaries while
maintaining a low public profile.

5. Long-Term Flexibility Through Successor Provisions

The Sigma Trust can be designed to evolve over time by
establishing **successor provisions** that ensure the trust
continues to function smoothly across generations. By
planning for the future, the principal can ensure that the
trust remains aligned with the principal's goals, even
after they pass on.

Key Successor Provisions:

- **Successor Trustees and Beneficiaries**: The trust
can specify how **successor trustees** will be
appointed in the event the current trustee is
unable or unwilling to serve. These provisions
ensure continuity in the management and

protection of the trust's assets. Additionally, successor beneficiaries can be named to ensure that the principal's legacy is passed on to future generations in alignment with the trust's terms.

- **Incentive Structures for Successors**: To ensure that successors are motivated to uphold the trust's values and mission, incentive structures can be built into the trust. These incentives can include financial rewards or additional control over the trust's operations for beneficiaries who demonstrate the ability to manage the trust's assets effectively.

Conclusion

Customizing the Sigma Trust for maximum flexibility is a critical strategy for ensuring that it remains relevant, functional, and effective in the long term. By tailoring the trust's terms, asset structures, and privacy provisions, the principal can ensure that the trust adapts to changing circumstances, optimizes asset protection, and continues to fulfill its purpose in a way that aligns with both the principal's objectives and the beneficiaries' needs. Through strategic customization, the Sigma Trust becomes not only a powerful tool for asset protection but also a flexible and adaptive structure that serves its purpose well into the future.

Chapter 10: Legacy Planning and Long-Term Goals

Section 1: Ensuring the Trust's Continuity Beyond Your Lifetime

One of the most powerful aspects of the Sigma Trust is its ability to continue operating effectively after the principal's lifetime. Through careful planning and strategic design, the trust can ensure that assets, intellectual property, and financial resources are preserved, managed, and distributed according to the principal's wishes for generations to come. This section will focus on ensuring the trust's continuity beyond the principal's lifetime by establishing a clear legacy plan that addresses both the protection and utilization of assets, as well as the governance of the trust over time.

---

1. Establishing a Successor Trustee Plan

One of the most critical components of ensuring the trust's continuity is the selection of a successor trustee. The trustee plays an essential role in the management and administration of the trust, and it is crucial that the principal designates a reliable and capable individual or entity to take over this responsibility when the current trustee is no longer able to serve.

Considerations for Selecting a Successor Trustee:

- **Competence and Integrity**: The successor trustee must be someone who is competent in handling financial and legal matters, as well as someone with strong integrity to ensure that the trust is administered according to the principal's wishes. It is also essential that the successor trustee understands the objectives and philosophies of the trust, particularly when it comes to asset protection and long-term planning.
- **Successor Trustee's Powers and Limitations**: The principal can outline the specific powers of the successor trustee, including the ability to manage and distribute assets, make decisions regarding the intellectual property held in the trust, and adjust distributions to beneficiaries as necessary. However, it is also important to define any limitations on the successor's powers to prevent overreach and maintain the trust's integrity.
- **Successor Trustee Selection Process**: The principal should also include a process for selecting a successor trustee. This process can involve the nomination of potential candidates, a method for resolving disputes in the selection process, and instructions for how the successor

trustee will be appointed if the designated
successor is unable or unwilling to serve.

2. Creating a Trust Protector to Oversee the Trust's Long-Term Goals

A **trust protector** is a crucial figure in the long-term
governance of the Sigma Trust. This individual or entity
acts as an overseer and guardian of the trust, ensuring
that the terms and objectives of the trust are upheld, even
if circumstances change over time. The role of the trust
protector is especially important for maintaining the
trust's continuity when unforeseen events occur, such as
changes in tax laws, shifts in the principal's desires, or
the emergence of new beneficiaries.

The Role of the Trust Protector:

- **Adjusting the Trust's Terms**: The trust
  protector can be granted the authority to make
  adjustments to the terms of the trust when
  needed, without the necessity of going to court.
  This ensures that the trust can adapt to
  unforeseen legal, financial, or personal changes.
- **Ensuring Fiduciary Responsibility**: The trust
  protector can be responsible for monitoring the
  actions of the trustee and ensuring that they are

fulfilling their fiduciary duty. If the trust
protector sees that the trustee is not acting in the
best interests of the trust, they can take corrective
action to ensure the trust remains compliant with
its original intentions.

- **Protection Against Abuse or Mismanagement**:
The trust protector can intervene if they believe
the trust is being mismanaged or abused by any
parties, including the trustee or beneficiaries. The
trust protector acts as a safeguard to ensure that
the principal's wishes are always respected and
that the trust is preserved for future generations.

3. Successor Beneficiaries and Generational Wealth Planning

Ensuring the continuity of the trust beyond the
principal's lifetime also involves establishing clear
guidelines for the distribution of assets to **successor
beneficiaries**. These provisions allow for the long-term
growth and protection of the principal's wealth, ensuring
that future generations benefit from the assets and values
held within the trust.

Planning for Successor Beneficiaries:

- **Designation of Beneficiaries**: The principal can designate successor beneficiaries, including children, grandchildren, or charitable organizations. This designation can be based on specific criteria, such as the beneficiary's need for support, their role in the family or organization, or their alignment with the principal's values.
- **Preserving Family Legacy**: For families, the principal may want to ensure that future generations understand and uphold the values that guided the creation of the trust. This can be achieved by embedding specific instructions or establishing an educational framework within the trust, which could include provisions for financial literacy, family governance, or philanthropic endeavors.
- **Charitable Beneficiaries**: The principal can also designate charitable organizations as beneficiaries, ensuring that a portion of the trust's assets is allocated to causes that were important to the principal. This can create a lasting legacy of philanthropy, with distributions directed to these organizations as per the terms of the trust.

4. Incorporating Flexibility for Changing Needs

While a core component of the trust's continuity is to preserve the principal's wishes, it is also important to build in flexibility to address the changing needs of beneficiaries and the evolving nature of society. This flexibility allows the trust to stay relevant, effective, and in alignment with the principal's values over time.

Methods for Ensuring Flexibility:

- **Discretionary Distributions**: By establishing **discretionary distributions**, the trustee can adjust the amounts and timing of distributions to beneficiaries based on their individual needs or life circumstances. This gives the trust the ability to support beneficiaries through life events such as educational pursuits, medical expenses, or the purchase of a home.
- **Adjusting for Inflation and Changing Financial Conditions**: The trust can include clauses that allow for the adjustment of financial distributions based on inflation, changing economic conditions, or other relevant factors. This ensures that the trust's assets retain their purchasing power over time, and that beneficiaries continue to receive fair and adequate support.

- **Updating the Trust to Reflect Modern Needs**:
  As societal norms and legal frameworks evolve,
  the trust should have mechanisms in place to
  update or modify its terms, without
  compromising the core intent. This can include
  incorporating new forms of assets, such as digital
  currencies or intellectual property, or adjusting
  beneficiary requirements to align with evolving
  family dynamics or tax regulations.

5. Ethical Legacy Considerations

Finally, an essential part of legacy planning is ensuring
that the trust's actions align with the ethical standards
and values that the principal holds dear. The Sigma Trust
provides a framework for long-term ethical legacy
planning, emphasizing responsibility, accountability, and
sustainability in how assets are managed and distributed
over time.

Key Ethical Considerations:

- **Sustainable Wealth Management**: The trust can
  be structured to prioritize sustainable financial
  strategies, ensuring that wealth is preserved not
  just for the present but for future generations.
  This may involve environmentally conscious

investments or creating an ethical investment portfolio that aligns with the principal's values.

- **Ethical Beneficiary Guidelines**: The trust can also include ethical guidelines for beneficiaries, such as the requirement to use distributions for responsible purposes. This could encompass educational goals, social responsibility, or the support of charitable endeavors.
- **Continuing the Principal's Values**: To honor the principal's values, the trust can establish principles that govern how the trust's assets are managed, distributed, and used, such as principles of fairness, justice, and equality. This will ensure that the trust serves not only as a financial tool but also as a vehicle for perpetuating the principal's ethical and moral values.

Conclusion

Ensuring the Sigma Trust's continuity beyond the principal's lifetime is not just about the preservation of assets—it is about creating a lasting legacy that reflects the principal's goals, values, and vision. By planning for the appointment of successor trustees, establishing clear guidelines for beneficiary distributions, incorporating flexibility, and safeguarding ethical standards, the trust can remain effective for generations to come. With careful and thoughtful planning, the Sigma Trust can continue to protect and grow assets while fulfilling the principal's long-term objectives, ensuring a legacy that endures through time.

Section 2: Designating Successor Trustees and Beneficiaries

In order to ensure that the Sigma Trust operates effectively beyond the principal's lifetime, careful attention must be paid to the designation of **successor trustees** and **beneficiaries**. These provisions not only secure the continuity of the trust's operations but also maintain alignment with the original intentions and goals set by the principal. This section will explore the essential considerations in designating successor trustees and beneficiaries, ensuring that the trust remains operational, fair, and aligned with the principal's vision.

---

1. Designating Successor Trustees

The role of a **trustee** is central to the functioning of the trust. Therefore, selecting and appointing **successor trustees** is crucial for maintaining the integrity and direction of the Sigma Trust. A successor trustee must be chosen with care, considering their ability to manage the assets, adhere to the trust's terms, and act in the best interest of the beneficiaries.

- **Competence and Trustworthiness**: The successor trustee should possess a clear understanding of the trust's purpose, legal frameworks, and financial management. Their competence ensures that the trust operates smoothly even after the principal's death or incapacity. Trustworthiness is equally important, as they will hold significant fiduciary responsibility.
- **Qualifications and Experience**: Ideally, the successor trustee should have experience in financial management, law, or estate planning. In some cases, it may be beneficial to designate a professional trustee, such as a trust company or a qualified attorney, to ensure ongoing expertise in the trust's administration.
- **Contingency Plans**: It's important to have a contingency plan in case the initially designated successor trustee is unable or unwilling to serve. This can include the appointment of multiple successor trustees, an order of succession, or a method of selecting a trustee through the use of a trust protector or other oversight mechanisms.
- **Trustee's Powers and Limitations**: The powers and limitations of the successor trustee should be clearly defined within the trust document. This includes the authority to distribute assets, modify the trust terms, appoint advisors, or make other

significant decisions. However, limitations should be imposed to prevent abuse of power and ensure that the trustee's actions remain consistent with the trust's original intentions.

Steps for Designating Successor Trustees:

- **Nominating a Successor Trustee**: The principal can specify one or more individuals or institutions as successor trustees in the trust document. Clear criteria should be established for selecting the most appropriate candidate, and the principal can include instructions on the process if a trustee vacancy arises.
- **Alternate Trustees**: To avoid disruptions in the trust's administration, it is wise to name at least one alternate trustee in the event that the primary successor cannot fulfill their duties.
- **Reviewing the Successor Trustee Regularly**: Life circumstances change, and so do the capabilities and availability of potential successor trustees. It is important to review the selection periodically, particularly if changes occur in the trustee's personal or professional life.

2. Designating Successor Beneficiaries

The designation of **successor beneficiaries** ensures that the principal's wishes are upheld regarding the distribution of assets over time. Beneficiaries are the individuals, organizations, or entities that will receive benefits from the trust, and their designation is a critical element in the long-term success of the trust.

Key Considerations for Selecting Successor Beneficiaries:

- **Beneficiaries' Relationship to the Principal**: Successor beneficiaries should be selected based on their relationship to the principal, whether they are family members, business partners, or charitable organizations. It is essential that the principal's personal desires are respected in how the trust benefits these individuals or organizations.
- **Beneficiary Requirements and Expectations**: The principal may choose to outline specific requirements for beneficiaries to receive their share of the trust. This could include conditions such as achieving educational goals, demonstrating financial responsibility, or aligning with particular moral or ethical standards set forth by the principal.
- **Ensuring Equity and Fairness**: The trust should be structured to ensure that the needs of each

beneficiary are met. This could mean balancing monetary distributions with non-financial benefits, such as the maintenance of family properties or continued business operations.

- **Generation and Charitable Considerations**: In cases where the principal wishes to provide for future generations or charitable causes, the designation of **successor beneficiaries** may include both family members and charitable organizations. The trust can allocate a portion of its assets to charitable causes that were important to the principal, ensuring that their philanthropic legacy is continued.

Steps for Designating Successor Beneficiaries:

- **List of Successor Beneficiaries**: The principal can list the names of individuals or entities who are to inherit or receive distributions from the trust upon their death. For future generations, the principal might opt to use terms like "lineal descendants" or "descendants by blood" to ensure that the trust benefits children, grandchildren, and further generations.
- **Flexible Provisions for Changes**: The trust document can include provisions that allow the principal to revise or update the beneficiary list as life circumstances change. For example, the birth of new children, the adoption of family members, or the inclusion of new charitable

causes might prompt a review of the trust's beneficiary designations.

- **Contingency for Pre-deceased Beneficiaries**: In the event a designated beneficiary passes away before the principal, a contingency plan should be in place. This plan can specify whether the deceased beneficiary's share will be reallocated to other beneficiaries or whether the share will be held in trust for the next eligible person.

3. Beneficiary Rights and Responsibilities

Once successor beneficiaries are named, it is vital to define their rights and responsibilities under the terms of the trust. The rights of beneficiaries should be clearly outlined to ensure that they understand their entitlements, as well as the limits of their claims on trust assets.

Beneficiary Rights:

- **Right to Distributions**: Beneficiaries have the right to receive distributions from the trust in accordance with the terms set by the principal. This may include income from the trust's assets or distributions of principal under specific circumstances.

- **Right to Information**: Beneficiaries typically have the right to be informed about the trust's financial status and the actions of the trustee. This helps ensure transparency and accountability in the trust's administration.

Beneficiary Responsibilities:

- **Proper Use of Distributions**: Beneficiaries may be expected to use distributions for specific purposes, such as education, healthcare, or supporting their family. The trust can include guidelines for how beneficiaries should use the funds they receive to maintain the integrity of the principal's intentions.
- **Adherence to Trust Terms**: Beneficiaries must comply with the conditions set by the trust, which may include maintaining ethical standards, participating in trust management, or following any other specific instructions laid out by the principal.

---

4. Updating Successor Trustee and Beneficiary Designations

The process of designating successor trustees and beneficiaries is not static. As life circumstances evolve, the principal may wish to update these designations to reflect new priorities, relationships, or changes in the law. It is important to include a flexible mechanism within the trust for updating these provisions, ensuring that the trust remains aligned with the principal's intentions.

Methods for Updating Designations:

- **Amendments to the Trust Document**: The principal can amend the trust to reflect changes in the designation of trustees and beneficiaries. These amendments must be executed in accordance with the legal requirements for modifying the trust.
- **Trust Protector's Role in Updates**: The trust protector, as appointed in the trust, may also have the authority to assist in updating designations, ensuring that changes are made in line with the principal's broader goals.
- **Periodic Reviews**: Regular reviews of the trust by the principal or a trusted advisor can ensure that the designations remain appropriate, particularly if the principal's family or business structure changes.

Conclusion

Designating **successor trustees** and **beneficiaries** is one of the most important aspects of ensuring that the Sigma Trust operates seamlessly beyond the principal's lifetime. Through careful selection, clear guidelines, and periodic reviews, the principal can ensure that the trust's objectives are achieved and that the beneficiaries receive their rightful share in accordance with the principal's wishes. By thoughtfully addressing these designations, the trust can maintain continuity, protect the principal's legacy, and serve its purpose effectively over time.

Section 3: Passing Down Intellectual Property Rights and Assets

Passing down **intellectual property (IP) rights** and **assets** within the Sigma Trust is crucial for preserving the wealth and creative contributions of the principal while ensuring that these assets are managed effectively over time. This section will explore the strategies, legal considerations, and key mechanisms for transferring IP assets such as trademarks, copyrights, patents, and royalties to successor beneficiaries and trusts, ensuring a smooth transition that maintains the integrity and value of these intellectual property rights.

1. Understanding the Importance of Intellectual Property Transfers

Intellectual property is a valuable asset class, often generating ongoing revenue streams and contributing significantly to the overall wealth of the trust. The protection, transfer, and management of these assets require careful consideration to ensure their continued benefit to the trust and its beneficiaries.

Types of Intellectual Property to Transfer:

- **Trademarks**: Trademarks represent the brand identity of the principal and may be crucial to ongoing business operations. A trademark often serves as a symbol of goodwill and brand value, generating income through licensing or brand recognition.
- **Copyrights**: Copyrights protect creative works, such as books, music, art, or software. Transferring the rights to these works ensures that future royalties, licensing agreements, or usage rights continue to flow to the trust.
- **Patents**: Patents protect inventions and innovations. Passing down patents can generate ongoing licensing fees or sales of the patented products, making them a significant asset for the trust.

- **Trade Secrets**: Trade secrets, such as proprietary business processes or formulas, represent valuable intellectual capital. The trust can protect these assets and continue to profit from them.
- **Royalties**: Royalties from previously established works (books, music, patents, etc.) represent a stream of ongoing income. Properly structuring the flow of royalties into the trust is essential for ensuring continued financial support for the principal or beneficiaries.

2. Mechanisms for Transferring Intellectual Property to the Sigma Trust

To ensure the smooth transition of intellectual property to the Sigma Trust, it is essential to structure the transfer process clearly and legally. There are several methods for transferring IP assets to the trust, each of which serves specific purposes and provides varying levels of control and protection.

Methods of Transferring IP:

- **Assignment of Rights**: The principal can formally assign their rights to the trust through an **assignment agreement**. This legal document transfers ownership of the intellectual property, effectively making the trust the new holder of the rights. The assignment should specify which assets are being transferred, whether it's a one-time transfer or an ongoing arrangement, and the terms of royalty distributions.

- **Licensing Agreements**: In some cases, the principal may wish to retain certain rights while still allowing the trust to benefit from the intellectual property. A **licensing agreement** can provide a way to continue receiving income while the trust holds the right to use or distribute the IP. The terms of the licensing agreement should be clearly stated to ensure proper royalties and usage rights.

- **Creation of a Holding Entity**: For more complex IP portfolios, it may be beneficial to establish a separate **holding entity** (such as a company or LLC) that owns and manages the IP assets. The trust can then hold the ownership interests in the entity, effectively consolidating IP rights under a corporate structure.

- **Trust as Beneficiary of IP Income**: The principal can designate the trust as the beneficiary of ongoing income from intellectual property. This method ensures that the royalty streams, licensing revenues, and other forms of income generated from IP are directed to the trust, where they can be managed for the benefit of the beneficiaries.

- **Creation of a Testamentary Trust for IP Assets**: If the principal does not want to transfer IP rights during their lifetime, a **testamentary**

trust can be created within their will. This trust would come into effect upon the principal's death and would contain instructions for passing down the intellectual property to successors or beneficiaries.

3. Protecting Intellectual Property During the Transfer Process

When transferring intellectual property to the trust, it is important to ensure that the assets are protected against infringement, misuse, or disputes. Here are key strategies to safeguard IP during the transfer process:

Legal Protections for Transferred IP:

- **Maintain Registration**: For trademarks, copyrights, and patents, it is essential to ensure that the intellectual property is properly registered with the relevant authorities (such as the U.S. Patent and Trademark Office or the U.S. Copyright Office). The trust should be listed as the new owner of the IP in these records, ensuring that the rights are legally recognized and protected.
- **Secure Transfer Documentation**: All transfer agreements (assignments, licensing, or holding

entity agreements) should be carefully drafted and executed. Clear documentation provides evidence of the trust's ownership, helping to prevent challenges from third parties.

- **Monitor IP Use**: Once the intellectual property is transferred, it is important to monitor its use to ensure that it is not being infringed upon or misused. The trustee, or a designated IP manager, should regularly check for any unauthorized use and take appropriate legal action if necessary.
- **Trademark and Copyright Enforcement**: If the intellectual property is being infringed upon, the trust has the legal right to enforce the trademark or copyright. This may involve sending cease-and-desist letters, pursuing litigation, or entering into settlement negotiations to protect the value of the IP.
- **Use of Non-Disclosure Agreements (NDAs)**: In cases where trade secrets or confidential information is involved, the use of **NDAs** with employees, contractors, and partners is essential to prevent unauthorized disclosure or misuse.

4. Ensuring Continuous Revenue Flow from IP Assets

Once intellectual property is transferred into the Sigma Trust, it is important to establish processes that allow the trust to continue generating revenue from the IP assets. This ensures that the trust remains financially viable and capable of supporting its beneficiaries and maintaining the integrity of the principal's legacy.

Ongoing Revenue Strategies:

- **Royalty Distribution**: The trust should set up clear guidelines for how royalties and other income generated from IP assets will be distributed to the beneficiaries. These terms should align with the principal's original intentions and ensure that the trust remains financially stable.
- **Licensing Agreements and Partnerships**: The trust can enter into new licensing agreements or partnerships to further monetize the intellectual property. For example, the trust may license the IP to businesses or organizations that wish to use the assets in exchange for royalty payments or lump sum fees.
- **IP Portfolio Management**: The trust should have a strategy for managing its IP portfolio, ensuring that valuable assets are maintained and leveraged for maximum financial benefit. This could involve selling certain rights, creating derivative works, or collaborating with other entities to enhance the value of the IP.
- **Diversifying Revenue Streams**: While intellectual property may provide a substantial revenue stream, the trust should consider

diversifying its income sources by investing in other assets, such as real estate, securities, or businesses, to ensure long-term financial security.

Conclusion

Transferring intellectual property to the Sigma Trust is a powerful way to ensure that creative works and valuable assets continue to generate income and benefit future generations. By utilizing proper transfer methods, securing legal protections, and establishing revenue strategies, the trust can maintain the value and integrity of intellectual property while safeguarding the principal's legacy. Through careful planning and management, the trust ensures that the intellectual property remains an asset that serves both the trust's beneficiaries and the broader goals set forth by the principal.

Section 4: How the Sigma Trust Creates Generational Wealth

The Sigma Trust, through its unique structure and strategic management, is designed to create **generational wealth** for its beneficiaries while maintaining asset protection, legal compliance, and tax efficiency. This section explores the key mechanisms by which the Sigma Trust fosters long-term wealth accumulation and ensures that the principal's legacy endures for future generations. The strategies outlined here are focused on maximizing the value of assets, including intellectual property, investments, and income streams, ensuring that wealth is passed down to beneficiaries in a sustainable and secure manner.

1. Strategic Asset Allocation for Long-Term Growth

One of the core strategies of the Sigma Trust is the **strategic allocation of assets** to ensure long-term growth and wealth preservation. By diversifying investments and holding a range of income-generating assets, the trust can ensure that wealth is not only protected but also continually appreciated.

Key Asset Allocation Strategies:

- **Real Estate Investments**: The Sigma Trust can hold real estate properties that appreciate over time, providing rental income and long-term capital gains. This includes residential, commercial, or even agricultural properties. As the value of the properties increases, so does the trust's overall wealth.

- **Stock Market Investments**: The trust can invest in stocks, bonds, mutual funds, and exchange-traded funds (ETFs) to generate returns through dividends, capital gains, and interest. The trust's investment portfolio should be diversified to reduce risk while ensuring consistent growth.
- **Intellectual Property (IP)**: By transferring IP rights such as copyrights, trademarks, patents, and royalties to the trust, the principal can generate continuous income streams. These assets can increase in value over time as the intellectual property grows in demand or is licensed for various uses.
- **Alternative Investments**: The trust can also explore alternative investments like private equity, hedge funds, and commodities, which often provide higher returns and help hedge against market volatility.

2. Income Generation Through Royalties and Business Ventures

Income generation is a fundamental component of creating generational wealth through the Sigma Trust. By structuring income-generating assets such as **royalties** and **business ventures**, the trust can provide ongoing financial support for future generations while ensuring that the principal's creative works and intellectual property continue to yield revenue.

Generating Income from IP and Business Ventures:

- **Royalties**: Intellectual property such as books, music, inventions, or trademarks can be licensed to third parties, generating ongoing royalties. These royalties can be funneled directly to the trust, creating a continuous source of income. As the IP appreciates in value, the royalty payments may increase, creating greater wealth for the beneficiaries.
- **Business Ventures**: The Sigma Trust can hold interests in businesses that produce ongoing revenue streams. Whether through private business ownership or investments in public companies, these ventures can be structured to provide both short-term income and long-term growth. The trust can also explore creating new businesses or startups that generate profits through innovation and market demand.
- **Licensing and Franchise Models**: Licensing the intellectual property or business model owned by the trust can generate substantial revenue. By franchising or licensing a product, brand, or service, the trust can earn fees and royalties while retaining ownership of the core assets.

3. Asset Protection and Legal Safeguards to Preserve Wealth

To create and sustain generational wealth, it is essential that assets are protected from external threats, such as creditors, lawsuits, and administrative fraud. The Sigma Trust incorporates several **asset protection strategies** to safeguard wealth from potential risks, ensuring that the wealth accumulated remains intact for future generations.

Key Protections for Long-Term Wealth Preservation:

- **Irrevocability**: The Sigma Trust is irrevocable, meaning that once assets are transferred into the trust, they cannot be taken back or accessed by the principal. This ensures that the wealth remains under the control of the trust and is protected from personal creditors or legal claims against the principal.
- **Spendthrift Provisions**: The trust can include **spendthrift clauses**, which restrict beneficiaries from accessing the principal of the trust and prevent creditors from seizing assets. These clauses help ensure that wealth is not squandered and remains protected for future generations.
- **Asset Segregation**: The trust can segregate assets into different categories, such as intellectual

property, real estate, and investments, making it more difficult for outside entities to attack the trust's wealth as a whole. This creates a layered defense against lawsuits or claims.

- **Trust Protector**: The appointment of a **trust protector** can further enhance asset protection by overseeing the trustee's actions and ensuring that the trust is administered according to its terms. The trust protector can be given the authority to remove or replace trustees and enforce provisions that protect the trust's assets.

4. Education and Stewardship for Future Generations

Creating generational wealth requires more than just accumulating assets; it also involves preparing future generations to manage and grow that wealth responsibly. The Sigma Trust includes provisions for **education and stewardship** to ensure that beneficiaries understand the value of the assets they inherit and are equipped to manage them effectively.

Educational and Stewardship Provisions:

- **Trustee Education**: The trust can fund education programs for the trustees and beneficiaries, ensuring they are well-versed in managing wealth, investing wisely, and understanding the legal and financial intricacies of the trust. This education can include financial literacy, estate planning, and business management.

- **Mentorship Programs**: The trust can provide mentorship opportunities where older generations guide younger beneficiaries in handling their inherited wealth. These mentorship programs can help beneficiaries navigate challenges, such as market fluctuations, tax implications, and maintaining the value of the assets.
- **Performance Benchmarks**: To encourage responsible management, the trust can set performance benchmarks that beneficiaries must meet before accessing certain assets or distributions. This ensures that wealth is used wisely and that future generations contribute to the trust's ongoing success.
- **Philanthropic Involvement**: Encouraging beneficiaries to engage in **philanthropic** activities, either through direct donations or by supporting charitable causes, helps cultivate a sense of responsibility and long-term vision. This involvement fosters a stewardship mentality, ensuring that wealth is not just accumulated but also used for broader societal benefit.

Conclusion

The Sigma Trust creates **generational wealth** by
strategically allocating assets, generating ongoing
income through royalties and business ventures,
protecting assets from external threats, and fostering
responsible stewardship in future generations. By
combining these elements, the trust ensures that the
wealth created by the principal continues to grow and
support the principal's goals for their family or chosen
beneficiaries. This framework not only preserves wealth
but also provides a foundation for continued prosperity,
ensuring that the principal's legacy endures for years to
come.

Chapter 11: Building a Movement with the Sigma Trust

Section 1: Using the Sigma Trust as a Tool for Sovereignty

The Sigma Trust is not only a tool for personal wealth, protection, and legacy, but also a powerful instrument for asserting **sovereignty** in a world dominated by government oversight, financial institutions, and corporate interests. In this section, we explore how the Sigma Trust can serve as a means of reclaiming individual autonomy and asserting control over personal and familial assets, free from the influence of administrative agencies and the mechanisms of the state. By understanding the trust's potential for **sovereign protection**, individuals can create a movement aimed at achieving true independence and self-determination.

1. Defining Sovereignty in the Context of the Sigma Trust

Sovereignty, in its purest form, refers to the ultimate authority and autonomy of an individual or group. For centuries, the concept of sovereignty has been linked to nations and governments. However, in the modern era, the **Sigma Trust** allows individuals to assert a form of personal sovereignty that transcends governmental control and external influence. By establishing a trust with carefully crafted clauses, irrevocable protections, and asset shielding, individuals can separate themselves from the jurisdiction of administrative agencies and gain greater control over their resources and decisions.

Key Elements of Sovereignty Through the Sigma Trust:

- **Separation from the State**: The Sigma Trust allows individuals to legally and effectively separate themselves from the administrative systems that regulate citizenship, taxation, and government control. By transferring assets, including intellectual property, to the trust, individuals assert control over their financial and legal matters, free from the interference of government bodies.
- **Legal Protection from State Interference**: As a separate legal entity, the trust is insulated from

state actions that would normally affect an individual. This includes protection from lawsuits, creditors, and government seizures, which are common methods used by administrative agencies to control assets.

- **Self-Determination**: The structure of the Sigma Trust allows individuals to make decisions based on their values, priorities, and goals, rather than following the directives of governmental systems that may not align with their personal beliefs. This self-determination is a key aspect of sovereignty, ensuring that the individual remains the ultimate authority over their assets and decisions.

2. The Role of the Trustee in Sovereignty

The **trustee** plays a crucial role in upholding the principles of sovereignty within the Sigma Trust. In the context of sovereignty, the trustee is not just a manager of assets but also an **agent of autonomy**, working in alignment with the principal's vision of independence. The trustee must act in the best interests of the principal, ensuring that all trust provisions are upheld and that the individual's sovereignty is protected.

Trustee Responsibilities in Maintaining Sovereignty:

- **Independent Administration**: The trustee, being a distinct entity separate from governmental structures, ensures that the trust operates autonomously, outside of the reach of state institutions. This includes making financial decisions, managing assets, and ensuring compliance with the trust's terms, without the influence of external parties.
- **Enforcement of Trust Terms**: The trustee is responsible for enforcing the provisions that safeguard the principal's sovereignty, such as clauses related to asset protection, confidentiality, and administrative shielding. This helps to create a robust defense against encroachment by administrative bodies.
- **Dispute Resolution and Defense**: In the event of external challenges to the trust, the trustee must be proactive in defending the trust's integrity and sovereignty. This may include legally challenging administrative overreach, contesting attempts at asset seizure, or resisting legal action designed to undermine the principal's autonomy.

3. Building a Movement for Sovereignty Through Trusts

While the Sigma Trust is a personal tool, it also has the potential to serve as a foundation for **building a broader movement** centered around individual sovereignty and financial independence. By sharing the benefits of the Sigma Trust structure, individuals can form a collective of like-minded people committed to resisting government control, reclaiming their assets, and asserting their autonomy.

Steps to Building a Sovereign Movement:

- **Educating the Public**: The first step in building a sovereignty movement is educating others about the Sigma Trust and its potential to provide financial independence, legal protection, and sovereignty. Through workshops, publications, and other educational initiatives, the principles of self-determination and asset protection can be spread.
- **Creating Communities of Like-Minded Individuals**: Building a community of individuals who are committed to sovereignty allows for mutual support and the sharing of strategies to strengthen personal autonomy. These communities can provide legal assistance,

share resources, and amplify each other's voices in resistance to administrative control.

- **Advocating for Legal Reforms**: A movement based around the Sigma Trust could push for changes in existing laws that restrict personal sovereignty or facilitate administrative overreach. By mobilizing individuals who are already using the trust to assert their autonomy, the movement can advocate for reforms that further protect personal rights and resist unnecessary government intervention.
- **Networking with Legal and Financial Experts**: The movement can also work with legal and financial professionals who understand the nuances of the Sigma Trust and can provide expert guidance on its use. By collaborating with these professionals, individuals in the movement can ensure that their trusts are established correctly and that their sovereignty is fully protected.

---

4. Protecting and Expanding Sovereignty in the Future

As administrative systems evolve and continue to seek greater control over individuals, the need for sovereignty becomes increasingly important. The Sigma Trust offers **a dynamic solution** to these challenges, but it requires ongoing vigilance and adaptation to ensure that it remains effective. This section will explore how individuals and communities can **expand and protect** their sovereignty in the future, ensuring that the trust's protections remain intact as society changes.

Long-Term Strategies for Expanding Sovereignty:

- **Adaptability to Changing Laws**: The Sigma Trust must be adaptable to changes in laws, both at the local and global levels. By continually reviewing and adjusting the trust's provisions, individuals can ensure that the trust remains effective in protecting sovereignty, even in the face of evolving legal landscapes.
- **Global Cooperation for Sovereignty**: As the world becomes increasingly interconnected, the movement for sovereignty can expand globally. By networking with like-minded individuals across borders, a global network can be formed, creating a broader impact and stronger resistance to global governance structures that infringe on personal autonomy.
- **Engaging in Public Advocacy**: The future of sovereignty will depend on public advocacy and the ongoing push for reforms that protect personal autonomy. Engaging with policymakers, legal systems, and the media allows the movement to influence change on a larger scale, ensuring that the right to sovereignty remains protected for future generations.

Conclusion

The Sigma Trust serves as a powerful tool for sovereignty, enabling individuals to reclaim control over their lives, assets, and decisions. By separating themselves from governmental oversight, the trust allows principals to assert their autonomy and protect their wealth, all while maintaining legal and financial independence. Through education, advocacy, and strategic action, the Sigma Trust can be leveraged to build a movement centered around **individual sovereignty**, empowering people to resist external control and create a future where true autonomy is possible.

Section 2: Inspiring Others to Build Their Own Trusts

One of the most powerful aspects of the **Sigma Trust** is its potential to inspire a broader movement of individuals who seek autonomy, protection, and independence from the systems that govern them. By demonstrating the benefits of establishing their own trusts, individuals can create ripple effects that extend far beyond their own lives, empowering others to reclaim their financial and personal sovereignty. This section explores how to inspire others to take control of their future by building their own Sigma Trusts, spreading knowledge, and fostering a community of like-minded individuals committed to self-determination.

---

1. The Power of Personal Example

One of the most effective ways to inspire others is by being a living example of what is possible when one builds a trust that offers both legal protection and autonomy. When others see the success, freedom, and security that come from establishing a Sigma Trust, they are more likely to follow suit.

How to Lead by Example:

- **Transparency and Education**: Share your experience in establishing the Sigma Trust and the impact it has had on your life. Through personal stories, individuals can see the real-world benefits of trust formation, especially in areas like asset protection, tax efficiency, and protection from administrative overreach.
- **Public Speaking and Engagement**: Host seminars, webinars, or workshops to discuss the benefits of creating a trust. Speaking publicly about how the Sigma Trust has helped you safeguard assets, intellectual property, and

sovereignty can create curiosity and motivate others to take action.
- **Mentorship and Guidance**: Offer to mentor others who are interested in building their own trusts. Helping someone establish their own Sigma Trust can be an empowering experience and a way to strengthen the movement. By teaching others the technical and philosophical aspects of creating a trust, you build a network of people committed to the same goals of financial and personal sovereignty.

2. Creating a Movement Through Education

Educating others is the most foundational way to inspire them to build their own trusts. Through workshops, books, articles, and online resources, you can introduce the concepts and benefits of the Sigma Trust to a wide audience.

Educational Outreach Strategies:

- **Workshops and Seminars**: Organize educational events where you can explain the intricacies of the Sigma Trust, how it works, and how it can benefit individuals who wish to take control of their financial and legal lives. Whether in person or online, these events can be a critical tool for spreading awareness.

- **Online Content**: Use digital platforms—blogs, social media, YouTube, or podcasts—to create a wealth of educational content about the Sigma Trust. Offering free resources, guides, and instructional videos can serve as a gateway for people to learn more and feel confident in starting their own trusts.
- **Creating Resources**: Develop easy-to-understand guides, templates, or checklists that individuals can use to start their own trust. Make the process accessible by breaking down complex legal concepts into clear, actionable steps.
- **Case Studies and Success Stories**: Share success stories from those who have already built Sigma Trusts. Real-life case studies can demonstrate the tangible benefits of the trust in a way that resonates with potential adopters.

3. Building a Community of Sovereignty

The creation of a community can amplify the impact of the Sigma Trust movement. By surrounding yourself with like-minded individuals, you create a network of support and shared knowledge that empowers everyone involved.

Building a Network of Sovereign Individuals:

- **Forums and Discussion Groups**: Establish or participate in online forums, social media groups, or discussion platforms dedicated to sovereignty and asset protection. These spaces can be used to share ideas, ask questions, and offer support to others who are starting their own trusts.
- **Collaborations and Partnerships**: Partner with other individuals or organizations that promote financial freedom, legal independence, or sovereignty. By aligning with other movements or communities, you can increase visibility and encourage more people to join the Sigma Trust movement.
- **Sovereignty Events and Meetups**: Organize local or virtual meetups for those interested in building Sigma Trusts. These events provide a sense of camaraderie and support, making it easier for individuals to take the step toward building their own trust.
- **Building an Advocacy Network**: Form alliances with legal and financial professionals who are sympathetic to the idea of personal sovereignty and independence. A strong network of experts can help those starting out with the trust process and lend credibility to the movement.

4. Empowering Others to Take Control

Inspiring others to build their own Sigma Trusts ultimately comes down to empowerment—giving people the tools, resources, and support they need to take control of their lives and assets. By showing others how easy it can be to regain sovereignty over personal wealth, intellectual property, and other assets, you create a ripple effect that can change the financial and legal landscape for generations to come.

Empowerment Strategies:

- **Offering Tools and Resources**: Make the tools and information needed to create a trust accessible and user-friendly. By providing templates, checklists, and easy-to-follow guides, you remove barriers that may intimidate or discourage others from creating their own trusts.
- **Encouraging Self-Discovery and Autonomy**: Inspire people to think critically about their own financial and legal situations. Encourage them to explore options for asset protection, wealth building, and sovereignty, and show them how the Sigma Trust can be a solution that aligns with their personal goals.
- **Support in Overcoming Legal Obstacles**: Help others navigate the legal aspects of building their trust. By offering guidance on how to work with attorneys, legal experts, or trustees, you ensure

that people don't feel overwhelmed or confused by the process.
- **Highlighting the Benefits of Ownership**: Reinforce the idea that the Sigma Trust allows individuals to take full ownership of their financial destinies. Show that by building a trust, they're taking back control and distancing themselves from the reliance on external systems that could limit their freedom and prosperity.

Conclusion

Inspiring others to build their own Sigma Trust is not just about offering a financial tool—it's about igniting a movement that fosters self-sufficiency, financial independence, and personal sovereignty. By leading by example, creating educational opportunities, and building a supportive community, you can empower individuals to take control of their financial and legal futures. As more people create their own Sigma Trusts, the movement for personal sovereignty grows stronger, creating a ripple effect that can change lives and reshape the future of individual rights and freedoms.

Section 3: The Sigma Trust as a Model for Social and Economic Reform

The **Sigma Trust** offers not only an individual path to sovereignty, asset protection, and financial independence but also serves as a powerful model for larger-scale social and economic reform. As individuals adopt the principles and structure of the Sigma Trust, they can collectively foster a paradigm shift in the way wealth, legal authority, and personal freedoms are understood and exercised. This section explores how the Sigma Trust can inspire broader societal and economic changes, challenging existing systems and providing an alternative framework for social and economic organization.

---

1. Reclaiming Sovereignty: The Foundation of Reform

At the heart of the **Sigma Trust** is the concept of sovereignty—the idea that individuals have the right to control their assets, their future, and their legal standing without undue interference from governmental or corporate systems. As more people build their own Sigma Trusts, they reclaim personal sovereignty and resist the influence of external systems that may seek to control or limit their freedoms. This model can inspire a broader movement for individual and collective sovereignty, challenging the traditional structures that often infringe upon personal rights.

How the Sigma Trust Promotes Sovereignty:

- **Financial Independence**: By protecting assets and income streams from external control, individuals who establish Sigma Trusts reclaim their financial independence. This reduces reliance on external institutions such as banks, government assistance, or corporate structures that often dictate personal financial decisions.
- **Legal Autonomy**: The trust's ability to protect its creator (the principal) from administrative agencies and legal systems gives individuals more control over their legal status and the decisions that affect their lives. This autonomy creates a buffer from invasive policies and structures that often limit personal choice.
- **Personal Freedom**: With a Sigma Trust, individuals can assert their right to live without the restrictions and obligations imposed by traditional systems of governance. The trust structure allows individuals to organize their affairs in ways that best reflect their values, priorities, and needs.

2. Economic Empowerment and Wealth Redistribution

The **Sigma Trust** allows individuals to better manage their wealth and create opportunities for wealth redistribution in ways that benefit not just the trust's creator but also future generations. By decentralizing wealth and giving individuals control over their financial destinies, the trust serves as a model for creating a more equitable and decentralized economic system. This stands in stark contrast to the centralization of wealth and power in corporate and government structures.

How the Sigma Trust Promotes Economic Reform:

- **Wealth Redistribution**: Through the trust, individuals can redirect wealth towards philanthropic causes or community investments that foster long-term social and economic benefits. The ability to allocate funds without the interference of centralized authorities allows for a more equitable distribution of resources.
- **Economic Decentralization**: The trust structure empowers individuals to retain control over their financial resources, effectively decentralizing wealth and reducing the concentration of power in governmental or corporate entities. This shift from centralized economic systems to

decentralized control promotes a more inclusive and diverse economic landscape.
- **Creating Alternative Economic Systems**: By utilizing the Sigma Trust to bypass traditional economic and financial institutions, individuals can establish alternative systems for generating and distributing wealth. These systems can be more aligned with values such as fairness, sustainability, and community-driven growth, breaking free from the constraints of traditional capitalist structures.

3. A New Social Contract: Self-Governance and Autonomy

As individuals establish and maintain Sigma Trusts, they move toward a model of **self-governance**—an alternative to the current systems of governance that often involve top-down control and limited personal participation. In a system where trust structures are embraced by many, people will have more autonomy in organizing their social, financial, and legal affairs, creating a new form of social contract that prioritizes the rights and freedoms of individuals over the control of external authorities.

How the Sigma Trust Reframes Social Contracts:

- **Voluntary Participation**: The Sigma Trust operates on the principle of voluntary association, meaning individuals willingly enter into these agreements based on their own preferences and needs. This creates a social contract based on mutual respect for personal freedom rather than coercion or obligation.
- **Direct Governance**: In the context of a broader societal adoption of trust models, individuals can collectively form self-governed communities where decisions are made through mutual agreements rather than imposed from above. This directly challenges hierarchical models of governance, such as those in current nation-states, and paves the way for more localized, direct forms of governance.
- **Collective Autonomy**: As more individuals take control of their legal and financial destinies through the Sigma Trust, a collective sense of autonomy emerges. This autonomy is not just personal; it extends to entire communities, creating a web of independent yet interconnected individuals who can work together to support each other's goals and interests.

4. Challenging the Status Quo: A Path to Reform

The **Sigma Trust** is not merely an individual legal structure; it represents a challenge to existing societal and economic norms. By utilizing the trust to protect assets, reduce reliance on external systems, and assert control over personal and financial affairs, individuals are taking a stand against systems that have historically marginalized their rights. This shift encourages others to examine and question the legitimacy of the systems that control wealth, governance, and legal authority.

How the Sigma Trust Promotes Systemic Change:

- **Challenging Corporate and Governmental Overreach**: By circumventing traditional financial institutions and governmental agencies, the Sigma Trust presents a challenge to systems that have long enjoyed control over individuals' wealth and rights. Through widespread adoption, it can reduce the influence of external entities that often infringe upon personal freedoms.
- **Inspiring Legal and Institutional Reform**: As the Sigma Trust model gains traction, it has the potential to influence legal and institutional reform. Governments and corporations may be forced to adapt to a society where individuals increasingly assert control over their financial

and legal affairs. This pressure can lead to positive changes in the legal landscape, as outdated systems are reevaluated in light of new models of governance.

- **Fostering a Cultural Shift**: The rise of the Sigma Trust can also spark a cultural shift away from dependence on centralized power structures. It encourages individuals to embrace self-reliance, autonomy, and sovereignty, creating a more empowered and self-determined populace. As these values spread, they can lead to greater social and economic equity, paving the way for a new era of reform.

Conclusion

The **Sigma Trust** offers more than just a personal legal and financial structure—it provides a roadmap for systemic reform in both social and economic spheres. By embracing sovereignty, decentralizing wealth, and fostering self-governance, the Sigma Trust serves as a model for a new type of social contract and economic system. As individuals build their own trusts, they contribute to a broader movement that challenges existing power structures and paves the way for a more equitable, decentralized future.

Section 4: Final Thoughts: Securing Your Legacy with Confidence

As we conclude this exploration of the **Sigma Trust** and its potential to revolutionize personal sovereignty, asset protection, and social reform, it is essential to reflect on the lasting impact that building and managing such a trust can have on your life, your assets, and your legacy. By taking the steps to establish and properly manage a Sigma Trust, you are not merely securing your financial future; you are shaping a legacy of freedom, independence, and generational empowerment.

This section explores the importance of maintaining confidence in the trust's ability to protect your wealth, safeguard your rights, and ensure that your values persist long after you're gone. It discusses how the principles of the **Sigma Trust** can provide enduring protection against legal, financial, and administrative challenges while allowing you to remain fully in control of your estate and intellectual property.

1. Legacy Preservation: Ensuring Your Values Endure

A key aspect of any trust is its ability to serve as a vehicle for legacy preservation, ensuring that your wealth, intellectual property, and ideals are passed down to future generations. The **Sigma Trust** offers a robust framework for this purpose, allowing you to create a lasting influence beyond your lifetime. By funding the trust with assets, intellectual property, and clearly defined instructions, you can leave a legacy that aligns with your values and vision for the future.

Key Considerations for Legacy Preservation:

- **Passing on Values, Not Just Assets**: Through the structure of the Sigma Trust, you can ensure that not only your wealth is passed on but also the principles that guided you in life. The trust allows you to embed values such as sovereignty, financial independence, and self-governance within the trust's operational framework, shaping the way your successors will manage and build upon your legacy.
- **Generational Impact**: The Sigma Trust's multi-generational potential means that future generations can benefit from the assets and protections you've established. This allows you to contribute to a long-term legacy that transcends

your lifetime, potentially sparking positive changes in society, family, or business for many years to come.

- **Protecting Family and Loved Ones**: By naming successors and beneficiaries who share your vision and values, you can ensure that your family members or loved ones continue to enjoy the benefits and protections provided by the trust, even in the face of external threats or economic volatility.

2. Confidence in Your Legal and Financial Future

The Sigma Trust is designed to offer unparalleled protection from creditors, governmental interference, and administrative fraud. By putting your assets, intellectual property, and financial interests under the protection of the trust, you ensure that your wealth is secure and shielded from potential threats. The trust's irrevocability, combined with the sophisticated asset protection strategies employed, helps provide peace of mind, knowing that your financial future and legacy are safeguarded regardless of external circumstances.

Building Confidence Through Protection:

- **Shielding from External Threats**: The trust provides a layer of defense against lawsuits, claims, or other financial attacks. By establishing clear protections and clauses, including those that defend against fraud and creditor claims, the Sigma Trust creates a secure financial environment where your assets remain protected, even in challenging times.

- **Legal Safeguards for Your Intellectual Property**: Whether through copyrights, trademarks, or patents, your intellectual property is a critical asset that the trust can manage and protect. With legal clauses tailored to prevent infringement or misuse, you ensure that your work remains secure, and you maintain control over its distribution and monetization.

- **Tax Efficiency and Compliance**: The tax strategies integrated into the Sigma Trust help you maintain confidence in your ability to navigate complex tax laws while ensuring that you minimize liability and maximize asset growth. Your wealth is managed in a way that complies with all applicable laws while optimizing tax benefits and reducing the impact of unnecessary tax burdens.

3. Strategic Flexibility: Adapting to Future Challenges

The **Sigma Trust** is not a static structure; it is designed to be flexible and adaptable to future changes in your life circumstances, the law, or the economic environment. This adaptability ensures that the trust continues to serve your needs and goals, no matter how those evolve. With provisions for successor trustees, amendments to the trust, and the ability to shift focus or allocate resources, the Sigma Trust offers a dynamic solution for long-term financial security.

Key Elements of Strategic Flexibility:

- **Adapting to Life Changes**: The trust allows you to make adjustments as needed, whether it's shifting beneficiaries, redistributing assets, or even adapting to new laws or regulations. This flexibility ensures that the Sigma Trust remains aligned with your intentions throughout your life.
- **Long-Term Planning with Confidence**: By taking a proactive approach to legacy planning and incorporating flexibility into the trust, you can ensure that your plans for the future remain on track, even if the landscape changes. Whether it's new business ventures, investments, or changes in family structure, the Sigma Trust provides the tools to maintain control.

- **Ongoing Oversight and Updates**: Through regular reviews and updates, the trust can evolve with your personal, financial, and legal needs. Designating trusted advisors or appointing a trust protector to oversee the trust's administration can provide you with ongoing guidance and reassurance, ensuring that your legacy remains intact and your goals are met.

4. Empowering Future Generations

The **Sigma Trust** isn't just a tool for asset protection; it is an instrument of empowerment. By transferring wealth, intellectual property, and decision-making power to future generations, you lay the groundwork for future leaders who will continue your mission of sovereignty, independence, and personal freedom. You are not only securing your financial legacy but also fostering a mindset of autonomy and responsibility in those who follow.

Ways the Sigma Trust Empowers Future Generations:

- **Educating Successors**: As you pass down your wealth and values, the trust offers an opportunity to educate future generations on how to manage, grow, and protect the assets entrusted to them. This education can inspire a new generation of self-reliant individuals capable of navigating the complexities of modern life with confidence.

- **Building a Lasting Social and Economic Impact**: The legacy you create through the Sigma Trust can extend beyond your immediate family or circle of beneficiaries. By supporting initiatives, causes, or projects that align with your values, you can contribute to a broader movement for societal and economic reform, empowering generations to come.
- **Strengthening Family and Community Ties**: The trust can serve as a tool to foster cooperation and mutual support among your family or community members, creating a network of individuals united by shared values and goals. This network can provide strength, security, and solidarity in the face of external challenges.

Conclusion: The Enduring Legacy of the Sigma Trust

The **Sigma Trust** offers a pathway to financial independence, legal sovereignty, and long-term legacy preservation. By securing your assets, protecting your intellectual property, and establishing a clear and flexible framework for wealth management, you can build a foundation for future generations that is resilient, sustainable, and aligned with your personal values.

As you consider the potential of the Sigma Trust, remember that the legacy you create is not only about what you leave behind but also about how you live today—empowered, protected, and confident in your ability to shape your future. Through the Sigma Trust, you secure not just wealth, but the very principles of sovereignty and freedom that will continue to guide and inspire those who come after you.

Appendices

Appendix A: Sample Trust Agreement Template

The following is a sample template for creating a **Sigma Trust Agreement**. This document provides a foundational framework for establishing the trust, detailing key roles, responsibilities, and provisions that can be customized to meet the specific needs of the trust's creator and beneficiaries. This template should be used as a starting point and modified according to legal advice to ensure compliance with applicable laws and regulations.

Sigma Trust Agreement

This Agreement is made and entered into on this [Date], by and between:

Settlor: [Name of Settlor]
Trustee: [Name of Trustee]
Beneficiaries: [Name(s) of Beneficiary(ies)]
Trust Protector: [Name of Trust Protector, if applicable]

Preamble

Whereas, the Settlor desires to create and fund a trust to be known as the **Sigma Trust** (hereafter referred to as the "Trust") for the purpose of providing asset protection, managing income and royalties, and ensuring the continuity of sovereignty, independence, and legal protections for the Settlor and the Beneficiaries.

Article I: Establishment of the Trust

1. **Name of Trust**: The Trust shall be known as the "Sigma Trust."
2. **Date of Establishment**: This Trust Agreement shall become effective on [Date].
3. **Settlor**: The Settlor, being of sound mind, hereby establishes this irrevocable trust and contributes the assets described in Schedule A.
4. **Trustee**: The Trustee shall manage the Trust according to the terms outlined in this Agreement. The initial Trustee is [Trustee Name]. The Trustee's powers,

responsibilities, and authority are outlined in Article II of this Agreement.

5. **Beneficiaries**: The Beneficiaries of this Trust shall be [Name(s) of Beneficiary(ies)] as defined in Schedule B.

6. **Trust Protector**: The Trust Protector is appointed to oversee the execution of the Trust's terms and provide supervision to ensure the Trust's intentions are carried out. The initial Trust Protector is [Name of Trust Protector].

Article II: Roles and Responsibilities

1. **Settlor's Role**:
   - The Settlor retains the right to modify certain provisions of the Trust during their lifetime.
   - The Settlor shall contribute assets, including intellectual property, real

estate, investments, and income streams, into the Trust.

2. **Trustee's Role**:

   o The Trustee is responsible for managing the Trust assets, maintaining records, and distributing funds according to the terms set out in this Agreement.

   o The Trustee shall ensure the proper management of income from intellectual property, royalties, and investments in accordance with the terms of the Trust.

3. **Beneficiaries' Role**:

   o The Beneficiaries are entitled to receive distributions from the Trust based on the terms and conditions outlined in this Agreement.

   o The Beneficiaries must comply with the Trust's governing principles, including the protection of intellectual

property and adherence to the
Settlor's legacy.

4. **Trust Protector's Role**:
   - ○ The Trust Protector is empowered to modify the Trust to ensure its continuity and compliance with the Settlor's goals.
   - ○ The Trust Protector can oversee the Trustee's actions to ensure fiduciary duties are upheld and safeguard against administrative fraud.

Article III: Funding the Trust

1. Initial Funding:
   - ○ The Settlor contributes the following assets to the Trust at the time of execution: [List of Assets, including intellectual property, royalties, real estate, investments, etc.].
2. Continuous Contributions:

- The Trust shall receive continuous contributions, including royalties, income, and other assets as they are generated. These contributions are intended to sustain and grow the assets under management.

Article IV: Asset Protection and Management

1. **Protection of Trust Assets:**
   - The assets held within the Trust are shielded from creditors, lawsuits, and other financial liabilities. The Trust is irrevocable and may not be altered except as explicitly allowed by the terms of this Agreement.
2. **Intellectual Property Management:**
   - Intellectual property held within the Trust, including trademarks, copyrights, patents, and other

intangible assets, shall be managed in
the best interest of the Trust and its
Beneficiaries. The Trust has the
authority to license, sell, or otherwise
monetize these assets.

Article V: Distributions

1. **Distributions to Beneficiaries**:
   - The Trustee shall make distributions
     to the Beneficiaries based on the
     terms outlined in Schedule B, subject
     to the availability of funds and the
     legal and financial objectives of the
     Trust.
2. **Trustee's Discretion**:
   - The Trustee may exercise discretion
     in making distributions, particularly
     where it concerns the financial needs
     or best interests of the Beneficiaries.

However, the Trustee must act within the guidelines established by this Agreement.

Article VI: Protections Against Fraud

1. **Anti-Fraud Measures**:
   - The Trust has embedded anti-fraud clauses that protect it from fraudulent claims, administrative interference, and misuse of its assets. These measures ensure that the Trust's assets are not diverted or misappropriated.
2. **Trust Protector's Role in Fraud Prevention**:
   - The Trust Protector is responsible for ensuring that fraud prevention mechanisms are implemented and enforced, including the oversight of the Trustee's actions and the approval

of any significant changes to the
Trust.

Article VII: Trust Continuity and Succession

1. **Successor Trustee**:
   - In the event of the death, incapacity,
     or resignation of the Trustee, a
     successor Trustee shall be appointed
     according to the provisions outlined in
     Schedule C.
2. **Successor Beneficiaries**:
   - The Trust's assets may be transferred
     to successor Beneficiaries as
     described in Schedule B. These
     successor Beneficiaries shall have the
     same rights as the original
     Beneficiaries.

Article VIII: Miscellaneous Provisions

1. **Governing Law:**
   - This Agreement shall be governed by and construed in accordance with the laws of [State or Country].
2. **Amendments:**
   - The Trust Agreement may be amended by the Settlor, provided the amendments do not violate the irrevocability clause of the Trust.
3. **Binding Effect:**
   - This Agreement shall be binding upon the Settlor, Trustee, Beneficiaries, and their respective heirs, successors, and assigns.

Signatures

Settlor:

[Name of Settlor]

Trustee:

[Name of Trustee]

Trust Protector:

[Name of Trust Protector]

Schedule A: List of Initial Trust Assets
[Include a detailed list of all assets transferred to the Trust.]

Schedule B: Beneficiaries
[Include names of all current and potential beneficiaries, and the percentage or type of interest in the Trust.]

Schedule C: Successor Trustee and Beneficiaries
[Include details on successor trustees and additional beneficiaries.]

This template is a starting point for creating your **Sigma Trust**. It's essential to work with a legal professional who can customize this template to fit your unique needs and ensure full legal compliance.

Appendix B: Glossary of Key Terms

This glossary provides definitions for key terms and concepts related to the **Sigma Trust** and trust law in general. Understanding these terms will help clarify the structure, function, and legal nuances of the trust.

---

1. Asset Protection

The legal strategies and mechanisms put in place to safeguard an individual's or entity's assets from creditors, lawsuits, or other financial liabilities. In the context of the Sigma Trust, asset protection is a key component in shielding trust assets from external claims.

---

2. Beneficiary

An individual or entity that benefits from a trust. In the Sigma Trust, the beneficiary is the person or group entitled to receive distributions from the trust as per the trust's terms.

3. Cestui Que Vie Trust

A trust in which the beneficiary is the person whose life determines the duration of the trust. The term "Cestui Que Vie" means "the person whose life it is" in Latin. This type of trust is commonly used to create a living trust for the benefit of a person while they are alive, with distributions and control structured around their lifetime.

4. Copyright

A form of legal protection granted to the creator of original works of authorship, including literary, artistic, and musical creations. Copyrights allow the creator or their designated assignee (such as a trust) to control the use and reproduction of their work.

5. Trust Protector

An individual or entity appointed to oversee and protect the interests of a trust's beneficiaries. The Trust Protector can make modifications to the trust to ensure that its terms are followed, provide oversight over the Trustee, and protect the trust from fraud or mismanagement.

6. Fiduciary Duty

A legal obligation of a fiduciary (such as a trustee) to act in the best interests of the beneficiaries. Fiduciaries must manage the trust's assets prudently, avoid conflicts of interest, and ensure transparency in their actions.

7. Irrevocable Trust

A type of trust that cannot be changed, modified, or revoked by the settlor once it is established. In an irrevocable trust, assets are transferred out of the settlor's estate, providing potential benefits such as asset protection and tax advantages.

8. Royalties

Payments made to the owner of a property or intellectual asset (such as patents, copyrights, or trademarks) for the use or licensing of those assets. In the Sigma Trust, royalties from intellectual property assets may be a significant income stream for the trust.

9. Trustee

An individual or entity appointed to manage the assets of a trust according to the terms outlined in the trust agreement. The trustee has the legal responsibility to act in the best interests of the beneficiaries, manage the assets prudently, and make distributions as specified.

10. Principal

The person or entity that creates and funds a trust. The principal may also be referred to as the settlor or grantor. In the Sigma Trust framework, the principal is the higher authority—often conceptualized as God or a guiding principle—and represents the source of trust management.

11. Agent

An individual or entity authorized by the principal or trustee to act on their behalf in certain circumstances. An agent in the context of a trust may carry out specific tasks under the direction of the trustee or principal.

12. Testamentary Trust

A trust that is created according to the instructions provided in a person's will and comes into effect upon their death. Unlike an irrevocable living trust, a testamentary trust is established after the settlor's passing.

13. Tax Exemption

A status granted to certain entities, such as trusts, that allows them to be exempt from certain taxes, like income or property tax. Tax-exempt trusts are subject to specific criteria and regulations that prevent abuse and ensure they serve charitable or other exempt purposes.

14. Trademark

A legally registered symbol, word, or other identifiers used to distinguish goods or services from others. The Sigma Trust can own trademarks, and protect the rights to these intellectual properties through proper registration and management.

15. Trust Agreement

The legal document that establishes the terms and conditions of a trust, including its purpose, the roles of the trustee, beneficiaries, and other parties involved, and how the assets should be managed and distributed.

16. Trust Corpus (or Res)

The corpus, or res, refers to the body of assets held within the trust. These assets can include property, cash, investments, intellectual property, or other resources that are managed by the trustee on behalf of the beneficiaries.

17. Settlor

The person who creates a trust and contributes assets to it. The settlor is responsible for drafting the trust agreement and defining its terms. In the context of the Sigma Trust, the settlor may also be referred to as the principal or creator.

18. Sovereignty

The authority or control that an individual or entity exercises over themselves or their assets, often in contrast to external control by governments or other organizations. In the Sigma Trust context, sovereignty refers to the idea that the trust grants the settlor or principal autonomy over their own assets and legal matters.

19. Beneficiary Designation

The process of naming the individuals or entities that will benefit from a trust. This designation outlines how

the trust's assets will be distributed to the beneficiaries
according to the settlor's wishes.

20. Legal Fiduciary

A legal fiduciary is a person or institution that manages
assets on behalf of another party (such as a beneficiary)
and is legally bound to act in the best interests of the
beneficiary.

21. Multi-Capacity Trust

A structure in which an individual (or entity) assumes
multiple roles within a trust, such as settlor, trustee, and
beneficiary. These roles can be designed to provide
comprehensive control, flexibility, and protection for the
assets within the trust.

22. Social Security Trust Fund

A U.S. government fund that provides benefits to
eligible individuals and their families, funded by payroll
taxes. In the context of the Sigma Trust, the Social

Security Trust Fund may be referenced when discussing strategies for transferring or protecting benefits under administrative management.

23. Living Trust

A trust established by the settlor during their lifetime. A living trust can be revocable or irrevocable, and it allows for the management and distribution of assets before the settlor's death, often avoiding probate.

24. Estate Planning

The process of arranging for the management and distribution of an individual's assets after their death. Estate planning often involves the creation of trusts, wills, and other legal instruments to ensure that a person's assets are distributed according to their wishes and in the most efficient manner possible.

25. Fraudulent Conveyance

The illegal transfer of assets or property with the intent to defraud, delay, or hinder creditors. In the context of the Sigma Trust, safeguarding against fraudulent conveyance ensures that assets placed into the trust are protected from being improperly transferred or claimed.

---

26. Successor Trustee

An individual or entity designated to take over the management of the trust in the event that the original trustee is unable or unwilling to continue fulfilling their duties. The successor trustee must follow the terms of the trust as outlined in the trust agreement.

This glossary is intended to clarify the terms and concepts central to the structure and operation of the **Sigma Trust**, helping readers better understand the mechanics, legal considerations, and protections associated with this trust model.

Appendix C: Recommended Resources and Tools

This appendix offers a curated list of resources and tools that will aid in the establishment, management, and understanding of the **Sigma Trust**. These resources cover legal, financial, tax, intellectual property, and administrative aspects related to trusts and asset protection.

---

1. Legal Resources

- **Nolo's Trusts & Estates Section**
  A comprehensive guide for individuals looking to understand and create various types of trusts. Nolo's articles and books cover everything from the basics of trusts to advanced strategies for asset protection and estate planning.
  Nolo Trusts & Estates
- **LegalZoom**
  An online platform that helps individuals and businesses create legal documents, including trusts, wills, and other estate planning instruments. LegalZoom also offers affordable consultations with licensed attorneys for personalized guidance.
  LegalZoom

- **American Bar Association (ABA) Trust & Estates Section**
  A professional resource for attorneys and individuals interested in the legal aspects of trusts, estate planning, and asset protection. The ABA offers articles, webinars, and resources on trusts and related subjects.
  ABA Trust & Estates
- **The Uniform Trust Code (UTC)**
  The UTC is a model law adopted by most U.S. states that provides guidelines for the administration of trusts. It's an essential reference for understanding trust law and regulations in the U.S.
  Uniform Trust Code (UTC)

---

2. Financial and Tax Tools

- **TurboTax Business**
  An excellent tool for managing trust tax filings, including preparing and filing tax returns for irrevocable trusts. It offers guidance on deductions, credits, and other tax-saving strategies.
  TurboTax Business
- **IRS Trust Tax Forms and Instructions**
  A critical resource for understanding and filing taxes related to trusts. It includes the necessary forms for trust taxation, including Form 1041

(U.S. Income Tax Return for Estates and Trusts) and related instructions.
IRS Trust Tax Forms

- **Wealthfront**
A robo-advisor platform that can be used to manage trust assets through automated financial planning. It offers personalized investment strategies and tools for tax-efficient management of trust funds.
Wealthfront

- **IRS Publication 950: Introduction to Estate and Gift Taxes**
This publication provides a thorough overview of estate and gift tax considerations when establishing and managing a trust. It's useful for understanding the tax implications of transferring assets into and out of the trust.
IRS Publication 950

---

3. Intellectual Property Management Tools

- **USPTO: United States Patent and Trademark Office**
The official government site for registering and managing trademarks and patents. It offers resources on trademark searches, applications, and maintenance.
USPTO

- **Copyright.gov**
  The official site for registering copyrights in the United States. It provides resources for individuals and entities looking to protect their creative works through copyright registration.
  Copyright.gov
- **IPWatchdog**
  A leading resource for intellectual property news, advice, and updates. IPWatchdog is particularly useful for staying informed about legal and regulatory changes related to trademarks and copyrights.
  IPWatchdog
- **LegalZoom Intellectual Property Protection**
  Offers affordable services for registering trademarks, patents, and copyrights. LegalZoom provides a straightforward process for protecting intellectual property assets through legal filings.
  LegalZoom IP Protection

4. Administrative Protection and Fraud Prevention

- **Trust Protector Services**
  An independent third-party entity that can be appointed to oversee and protect the interests of a trust's beneficiaries. Trust protector services can be vital in ensuring the trust's terms are respected and that fraudulent activities are prevented.
  Trust Protector Services

- **Fraud Prevention Software: Experian**
  Experian offers fraud protection services that help safeguard personal and trust assets against identity theft and financial fraud. It's useful for monitoring the integrity of trust accounts and managing risk.
  Experian Fraud Prevention
- **The Fair Debt Collection Practices Act (FDCPA)**
  A key law that governs the practices of debt collectors. Understanding the FDCPA can help protect trust assets from creditor claims and fraudulent activities targeting beneficiaries.
  FDCPA
- **Financial Fraud Enforcement Task Force (FFETF)**
  A government-led task force aimed at preventing and investigating financial fraud. The FFETF provides resources and guidelines for addressing administrative fraud, which could be valuable when protecting the trust's assets.
  FFETF

---

5. Estate Planning Resources

- **Estate Planning Basics (Nolo)**
  Nolo's estate planning section offers helpful articles, guides, and templates for creating wills, trusts, and other estate planning documents. It is

a solid resource for understanding how to structure the Sigma Trust in the broader context of estate planning.
Estate Planning Basics

- **The Wealth Counsel**
  A resource for creating comprehensive estate planning strategies that incorporate various tools like trusts, family limited partnerships, and other advanced wealth management techniques.
  Wealth Counsel

- **The American College of Trust and Estate Counsel (ACTEC)**
  A professional organization of estate planning attorneys that provides information, resources, and referrals for individuals seeking expert advice on trust law and asset protection.
  ACTEC

- **The Living Trust Network**
  A website offering information on how to create and manage living trusts, including step-by-step guides and links to trusted legal professionals who can help with setting up the Sigma Trust.
  Living Trust Network

---

6. General Trust and Legal Forms

- **Rocket Lawyer**
  An online legal service that provides customizable trust documents, including

irrevocable trusts and other legal forms. It also
offers affordable consultations with attorneys.
Rocket Lawyer
- **Trusts & Estates Legal Forms (LawDepot)**
  LawDepot provides a variety of customizable
  trust forms and estate planning documents. These
  can be helpful for creating a trust that aligns with
  the Sigma Trust's framework and objectives.
  LawDepot Trust Forms
- **FindLaw: Trusts**
  A comprehensive legal resource that provides
  free articles, guides, and state-specific laws on
  trusts and estates. FindLaw is particularly useful
  for understanding the different types of trusts and
  their legal implications.
  FindLaw Trusts

Conclusion

These recommended resources and tools offer valuable
guidance for effectively establishing, managing, and
protecting the **Sigma Trust**. Whether you are navigating
the complexities of trust law, ensuring tax compliance,
or protecting intellectual property, these resources
provide the necessary knowledge and tools to manage
the trust successfully and ethically.

Appendix D: Case Studies and Success Stories

This appendix highlights real-world examples and success stories from individuals and organizations who have successfully used trust structures similar to the **Sigma Trust** to achieve asset protection, tax efficiency, and legal safeguards. These case studies are designed to illustrate how the Sigma Trust model can be applied in various scenarios, showcasing its versatility and effectiveness.

---

1. Case Study 1: The Successful Protection of Intellectual Property Assets

Background:
John, a tech entrepreneur, had developed a groundbreaking software platform that was gaining significant market traction. As his business grew, he became increasingly concerned about the potential for intellectual property theft, lawsuits, and the growing scrutiny from administrative agencies.

Solution:
John established an irrevocable **Sigma Trust** to protect his intellectual property assets, which included

copyrights and trademarks related to the software. By
transferring the ownership of these assets into the trust,
John was able to shield them from creditors and reduce
the risk of infringement.

Outcome:
The trust provided a solid legal structure that
safeguarded John's intellectual property from being
seized in the event of a lawsuit or creditor claim. It also
allowed him to pass the ownership of his intellectual
property to beneficiaries, ensuring that it would remain
protected for future generations. His business continued
to flourish without the constant fear of administrative
and legal risks.

---

2. Case Study 2: Using the Sigma Trust for Tax

Efficiency

Background:
Sarah, a successful author, was receiving substantial
royalty payments from her books, but the high tax
burden on her personal income was limiting her financial
growth. She was concerned about how to preserve her
wealth for future generations while minimizing the
impact of taxes.

Solution:
Sarah created a **Sigma Trust** and transferred her book

royalties into it. By doing so, she was able to take advantage of the tax exemptions and efficiencies associated with irrevocable trusts. The trust was structured to generate income streams that were taxed at a lower rate than her personal income.

Outcome:
The **Sigma Trust** allowed Sarah to reduce her taxable income while still enjoying the financial benefits of her royalties. The trust also ensured that her royalties would continue to be passed down to future generations with minimal tax liability. Sarah was able to grow her wealth more efficiently, creating a legacy that would last for decades.

---

3. Case Study 3: Shielding Family Assets from Administrative Fraud

Background:
A family living in a high-risk legal environment, where government agencies were known to engage in fraud and asset confiscation, was looking for a way to protect their family estate from these threats. The family wanted to preserve their wealth for future generations while protecting themselves from administrative overreach.

Solution:
The family established a **Sigma Trust**, with the principal

assets of their estate transferred into the trust. They also included a **Trust Protector** clause to oversee the trust's management and ensure that no unauthorized access could be made to the assets. The family's assets were shielded from administrative actions, including asset forfeiture.

Outcome:
By utilizing the **Sigma Trust** structure, the family was able to safeguard their wealth from potential fraud and abuse by government agencies. The Trust Protector's oversight provided an additional layer of protection, ensuring that no external party could interfere with the trust's operations. The family was able to continue living with peace of mind, knowing their assets were secure.

---

4. Case Study 4: Managing Royalty Streams for

Beneficiaries

Background:
David, a musician, had accumulated significant royalty streams from his music catalog. He wanted to ensure that these royalties were managed effectively for his beneficiaries (his children and grandchildren), while also protecting the assets from claims by third parties.

Solution:
David established a **Sigma Trust**, transferring his music

catalog and associated royalties into the trust. The trust
was structured to distribute royalties to his beneficiaries
on a periodic basis, ensuring they had financial support
while maintaining the integrity of the assets. David also
ensured that the trust provided protections against
creditors and third-party claims.

Outcome:
David's family continued to benefit from the royalties,
with regular distributions to the beneficiaries. The **Sigma
Trust** ensured that the royalties were protected from
creditors and lawsuits. The assets remained intact for
future generations, fulfilling David's goal of providing
financial security and legacy to his family.

---

5. Case Study 5: Protecting Personal Assets from Creditor Claims

Background:
Robert, a small business owner, faced a significant risk
of legal action from a disgruntled customer, which could
potentially result in the seizure of his personal assets. He
wanted a way to shield his assets from creditors while
maintaining control of his business and personal wealth.

Solution:
Robert created an irrevocable **Sigma Trust**, placing his
personal assets, including his home, investments, and

savings, into the trust. The trust's structure ensured that the assets were legally protected from seizure by creditors. Robert continued to manage his business and assets as the trustee, but the assets themselves were held by the trust, providing a layer of legal protection.

Outcome:
When the legal claim was filed, the trust's assets were not subject to seizure, protecting Robert's personal wealth. The trust structure allowed Robert to continue running his business while safeguarding his assets from future risks. The trust also ensured that his family would inherit his wealth without facing creditor claims.

6. Case Study 6: Transferring Social Security Benefits Into a Trust

Background:
Nancy, a retiree, was concerned about her Social Security benefits being subject to administrative fraud or mismanagement. She wanted to ensure that her benefits were protected and passed on to her heirs without the interference of external parties.

Solution:
Nancy established a **Sigma Trust**, transferring her Social Security benefits directly into the trust. By doing so, she ensured that her benefits would be protected from

administrative errors, fraud, and potential creditors. The trust was structured to allow for periodic distributions to Nancy while maintaining full control over her benefits.

Outcome:
Nancy was able to enjoy the security of knowing that her Social Security benefits were protected from outside claims and misuse. The trust provided her with peace of mind while ensuring that the funds were passed on according to her wishes, without the threat of fraud or misappropriation.

Conclusion:

The case studies and success stories featured in this appendix demonstrate the power and flexibility of the **Sigma Trust** structure. Whether it's for protecting intellectual property, managing royalty streams, shielding assets from creditors, or ensuring tax efficiency, the Sigma Trust has proven to be an effective tool for a wide range of individuals and organizations. By employing the trust's multi-capacity structure and legal safeguards, beneficiaries can secure their wealth and legacy while navigating the complexities of modern legal and financial landscapes.